Careers in Focus

HF5438.25 .C327 2009

0134112225922

Careers in focus.

c2009.

2009 11 12

Careers in Focus

SALES

Ferguson
An imprint of Infobase Publishing

Careers in Focus: Sales

Copyright © 2009 by Infobase Publishing

All rights reserved. No part of this book may be reproduced or utilized in any form or by any means, electronic or mechanical, including photocopying, recording, or by any information storage or retrieval systems, without permission in writing from the publisher. For information contact

Ferguson
An imprint of Infobase Publishing
132 West 31st Street
New York NY 10001

Library of Congress Cataloging-in-Publication Data

Careers in focus. Sales.
   p. cm.
   Includes index.
   ISBN-13: 978-0-8160-7308-5 (hardcover : alk. paper)
   ISBN-10: 0-8160-7308-2 (hardcover : alk. paper) 1. Selling. 2. Selling—Vocational guidance. I. Ferguson Publishing. II. Title: Sales.
   HF5438.25.C327 2009
   381.023—dc22
                            2009005165

Ferguson books are available at special discounts when purchased in bulk quantities for businesses, associations, institutions, or sales promotions. Please call our Special Sales Department in New York at (212) 967-8800 or (800) 322-8755.

You can find Ferguson on the World Wide Web at http://www.fergpubco.com

Text design by David Strelecky
Cover design by Jooyoung An

Printed in the United States of America

MP MSRF 10 9 8 7 6 5 4 3 2 1

This book is printed on acid-free paper.

Table of Contents

Introduction 1
Advertising Account Executives 5
Antiques and Art Dealers 12
Auctioneers 20
Automobile Sales Workers 29
College Professors, Sales and Marketing 39
Commodities Brokers 47
Computer and Electronics
    Sales Representatives 58
Counter and Rental Clerks 66
Financial Services Brokers 72
Insurance Agents and Brokers 78
Internet Store Managers and Entrepreneurs . . . 94
Internet Transaction Specialists 103
Purchasing Agents 112
Real Estate Agents and Brokers 120
Retail Sales Managers 128
Retail Sales Workers 135
Sales Managers 145
Sales Representatives 151
Services Sales Representatives 161
Wireless Sales Workers 168
Index 179

Introduction

Sales is a complex and diverse field. It involves the selling of all types of physical goods, such as automobile parts, pharmaceuticals, clothing, health care products, books, and food, as well as services, such as automobile repair or rug cleaning.

The selling of physical goods usually requires both a wholesaler and a retailer. The wholesaler is a go between, or person in the middle, between producers of merchandise and retail stores. The wholesaler buys goods in large quantities directly from producers, stores the goods in warehouses, takes orders from buyers (typically retail stores), and arranges for delivery of the merchandise.

The retail field consists of supermarkets, department stores, chain stores, specialty stores, variety stores, franchise stores, mail-order houses, and door-to-door sellers. Retail stores buy their goods from wholesalers, stock the goods, and resell them to individual consumers in small quantities. Retailers must know their customers' needs and wants, and they must also advertise and attractively display the goods they sell.

In the past few decades manufacturing of products has declined and the service industry has increased. Printing, pest control, telecommunications, computer maintenance, lodging, and transportation are among a huge variety of services that employ sales forces. Originally, services sales were accomplished through individual contact with potential buyers. That method is still used today, along with direct mail, telephone, the Internet, and print and media advertising. Both product sales and services sales are closely connected with the advertising, printing, mailing, transportation, and broadcast industries.

According to the U.S. Department of Labor, wage and salary jobs in wholesale trade are expected to grow about 7 percent through 2016, which is slower than the average for all industries combined. Industry trends in the next decade will include consolidation into larger firms and the spread of new technology, both of which should slow growth in some occupations.

Heightened competition and pressure to lower operating costs should continue to force mergers. The result will be reduced demand for some workers. More jobs should be available in customer services as consolidation and competition encourage expansion of these services. There also will be employment opportunities for workers in financial, logistical, technical, and advertising positions.

Electronic commerce and other types of new technology are expected to affect employment, particularly administrative support and marketing and sales positions. Those jobs are expected to decline as computer technology improves worker productivity. Much of the record keeping, ordering, and processing in wholesaling will be automated, as will inventory management, and shipping. E-commerce will lessen the need for bookkeeping, accounting, and auditing clerks. E-commerce will also affect sales workers. Inside sales workers' jobs will become more technology-dependent as they use computers to track inventory, solicit new business, and provide customer service. Outside sales workers' jobs will focus more on customer service.

The U.S. Department of Labor projects that employment for retail sales workers is expected to increase about as fast as the average for all occupations through 2016 due to anticipated growth in retail sales created by a growing population. There will continue to be many opportunities for part-time and temporary workers during peak selling periods. However, during economic downturns, sales decline and the demand for sales workers also declines.

The articles in *Careers in Focus: Sales* appear in Ferguson's *Encyclopedia of Careers and Vocational Guidance,* but have been updated and revised with the latest information from the U.S. Department of Labor, professional organizations, and other sources.

The following paragraphs detail the sections and features that appear in the book.

The **Quick Facts** section provides a brief summary of the career, including recommended school subjects, personal skills, work environment, minimum educational requirements, salary ranges, certification or licensing requirements, and employment outlook. This section also provides acronyms and identification numbers for the following government classification indexes: the Dictionary of Occupational Titles (DOT), the Guide for Occupational Exploration (GOE), the National Occupational Classification (NOC) Index, and the Occupational Information Network (O*NET)-Standard Occupational Classification System (SOC) index. The DOT, GOE, and O*NET-SOC indexes have been created by the U.S. government; the NOC index is Canada's career classification system. Readers can use the identification numbers listed in the Quick Facts section to access further information about a career. Print editions of the DOT (*Dictionary of Occupational Titles.* Indianapolis, Ind.: JIST Works, 1991) and GOE (*Guide for Occupational Exploration.* Indianapolis, Ind.: JIST Works, 2001) are available at libraries. Electronic versions of the NOC (http://www23.hrdc-drhc.gc.ca) and O*NET-SOC (http://online.onetcenter.org) are available on the Internet. When no DOT, GOE, NOC, or O*NET-SOC numbers are present, this means that the U.S. Department of Labor or Human Resources Development Canada have not created a numerical designation for this career. In this instance, you will see the acronym "N/A," or not available.

The **Overview** section is a brief introductory description of the duties and responsibilities involved in this career. Oftentimes, a career may have a variety of job titles. When this is the case, alternative career titles are presented. Employment statistics are also provided, when available. The **History** section describes the history of the particular job as it relates to the overall development of its industry or field. **The Job** describes the primary and secondary duties of the job. **Requirements** discusses high school and postsecondary education and training requirements, any certification or licensing that is necessary, and other personal requirements for success in the job. **Exploring** offers suggestions on how to gain experience in or knowledge of the particular job before making a firm educational and financial commitment. The focus is on what can be done while still in high school (or in the early years of college) to gain a better understanding of the job. The **Employers** section gives an overview of typical places of employment for the job. **Starting Out** discusses the best ways to land that first job, be it through the college career services office, newspaper ads, Internet employment sites, or personal contact. The **Advancement** section describes what kind of career path to expect from the job and how to get there. **Earnings** lists salary ranges and describes the typical fringe benefits. The **Work Environment** section describes the typical surroundings and conditions of employment—whether indoors or outdoors, noisy or quiet, social or independent. Also discussed are typical hours worked, any seasonal fluctuations, and the stresses and strains of the job. The **Outlook** section summarizes the job in terms of the general economy and industry projections. For the most part, Outlook information is obtained from the U.S. Bureau of Labor Statistics and is supplemented by information gathered from professional associations. Job growth terms follow those used in the *Occupational Outlook Handbook*. Growth described as "much faster than the average" means an increase of 21 percent or more. Growth described as "faster than the average" means an increase of 14 to 20 percent. Growth described as "about as fast as the average" means an increase of 7 to 13 percent. Growth described as "more slowly than the average" means an increase of 3 to 6 percent. "Little or no change" means a decrease of 2 percent to an increase of 2 percent. "Decline" means a decrease of 3 percent or more. Each article ends with **For More Information,** which lists organizations that provide information on training, education, internships, scholarships, and job placement.

Careers in Focus: Sales also includes photos, informative sidebars, and interviews with professionals in the field.

Advertising Account Executives

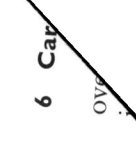

OVERVIEW

Advertising account executives coordinate and oversee everything related to a client's advertising account and act as the primary liaison between the agency and the client. They are also responsible for building and maintaining professional relationships among clients and coworkers to ensure the successful completion of major ad campaigns and the assurance of continued business with clients. Advertising account executives and related workers hold 170,000 jobs in the United States.

HISTORY

When the advertising industry formally developed in the late 1800s, advertisers themselves were usually the ones who handled the promotion of their products and services, placing ads in newspapers and magazines in order to reach their customers. As the number of newspapers increased and print advertising became more widespread, however, these advertisers called on specialists who knew how to create and coordinate effective advertisements. One such specialist, the advertising account executive, emerged to produce and handle the ad campaigns for businesses.

Advertising agencies were commonly used by companies by the 1920s, and account executives worked for such agencies. Together with a staff of creative professionals, the account executive was able to develop an advertising "package," including slogans, jingles, and images, as well as a general campaign strategy. In addition, account executives did basic market research,

---

QUICK FACTS

School Subjects
Business
English
Speech

Personal Skills
Communication/ideas
Helping/teaching

Work Environment
Primarily indoors
Primarily one location

Minimum Education Level
Bachelor's degree

Salary Range
$20,000 to $42,820 to $150,000+

Certification or Licensing
None available

Outlook
Faster than the average

DOT
164

GOE
10.02.02

NOC
1122

O*NET-SOC
41-3011.00

oversaw the elements that went into a campaign, and worked hand-in-hand with writers and artists to develop effective ads for their client companies.

Today, account executives handle all aspects of their clients' ad campaigns. As a result, they bring to the job a broad base of knowledge, including account management, marketing, sales promotion, merchandising, client accounting, print production, public relations, and the creative arts.

THE JOB

Account executives track the day-to-day progress of the overall advertising campaigns of their clients. Together with a staff commonly consisting of a creative director, an art director, a copywriter, researchers, and production specialists, the account executive monitors all client accounts from beginning to end.

Before an advertising campaign is actually launched, a lot of preparatory work is needed. Account executives must familiarize themselves with their clients' products and services, target markets, goals, competitors, and preferred media. Together with the agency team, the account executive conducts research and holds initial meetings with clients. Then the team, coordinated by the account executive, uses this information to analyze market potential and presents recommendations to the client.

After an advertising strategy has been determined and all terms have been agreed upon, the agency's creative staff goes to work, developing ideas and producing various ads to present to the client. During this time, the account executive works with *media buyers* (who purchase radio and television time and publication space for advertising) in order to develop a schedule for the project and make sure that the costs involved are within the client's budget.

When the ad campaign has been approved by the client, production can begin. In addition to supervising and coordinating the work of copywriters, editors, graphic artists, production specialists, and other employees on the agency team, the account executive must also write reports and draft business correspondence, follow up on all client meetings, interact with outside vendors, and ensure that all pieces of the advertising campaign clearly communicate the desired message. In sum, the account executive is responsible for making sure that the client is satisfied. This may require making modifications to the campaign, revising cost estimates and events schedules, and redirecting the efforts of the creative staff.

In addition to their daily responsibilities of tracking and handling clients' advertising campaigns, account executives must also develop and bring in new business, keep up to date on current advertising trends, evaluate the effectiveness of advertising programs, and track sales figures.

REQUIREMENTS

High School
You can prepare for a career as an advertising account executive by taking a variety of courses at the high school level. Basic courses in English, journalism, communication, economics, psychology, business, social science, and mathematics, are important for aspiring advertising account executives.

Postsecondary Training
Most advertising agencies hire college graduates whose degrees can vary widely, from English, journalism, or marketing to business administration, speech communications, or fine arts. Courses in psychology, sociology, business, economics, and any art medium are helpful. Some positions require a graduate degree in advertising, art, or marketing. Others may call for experience in a particular field, such as health care, insurance, or retail.

While most employers prefer a broad liberal arts background with courses in marketing, market research, sales, consumer behavior, communication, and technology, many also seek employees who already have some work experience. Those candidates who have completed on-the-job internships at agencies or have developed portfolios will have a competitive edge.

Other Requirements
While account executives do not need to have the same degree of artistic skill or knowledge as art directors or graphic designers, they must be imaginative and understand the communication of art and photography in order to direct the overall progress of an ad campaign. They should also be able to work under pressure, motivate employees, solve problems, and demonstrate flexibility, good judgment, decisiveness, and patience.

Account executives must be aware of trends and be interested in the business climate and the psychology of making purchases. In addition, they should be able to write clearly, make effective presentations, and communicate persuasively. It is also helpful to stay abreast of the various computer programs used in advertising design and management.

EXPLORING

Read publications like *Advertising Age* (http://www.adage.com), *Adweek* (http://www.adweek.com), and *Brandweek* (http://www.brandweek.com) to become familiar with advertising issues, trends, successes, and failures. Visit the Clio Awards Web site (http://www.clioawards.com). Clios are given each year in a variety of categories including television/cinema/digital, billboard, poster, radio, print: direct mail, interactive, and student work. The site also has information about advertising and art schools, trade associations, and links to some of the industry's trade magazines.

To gain practical business experience, become involved with advertising or promotion activities at your school for social events, sports events, political issues, or fund-raising events. If your school newspaper or yearbook has paid advertising, offer to work in ad sales.

EMPLOYERS

Approximately 170,000 advertising account executives work in the United States. Advertising agencies all across the country and abroad employ advertising account executives. Of the 19,200 full-service agencies in the United States, the large firms located in New York, Chicago, and Los Angeles tend to dominate the advertising industry. However, 68 percent of these organizations employ fewer than five people. These "small shops" offer employment opportunities for account executives with experience, talent, and flexibility.

STARTING OUT

Many people aspiring to the job of account executive participate in internships or begin as assistant executives, allowing them to work with clients, study the market, and follow up on client service. This work gives students a good sense of the rhythm of the job and the type of work required of account executives.

College graduates, with or without experience, can start their job search in their school's career services office. Staff there can set up interviews and help polish resumes.

The advertising arena is rich with opportunities. When looking for employment, you don't have to target agencies. Instead, search for jobs with large businesses that may employ advertising staff. If you want to work at an agency, you'll find the competition intense for jobs. Once hired, account executives often participate in special training programs that both initiate them and help them to succeed.

Mean Annual Earnings for Advertising Account Executives by Industry, 2007

Motion Picture and Video Industries	$63,290
Cable and Other Subscription Programming	$59,110
Advertising and Related Services	$56,710
Radio and Television Broadcasting	$53,640
Newspaper, Periodical, Book, and Directory Publishers	$45,610

Source: U.S. Department of Labor

ADVANCEMENT

Since practical experience and a broad base of knowledge are often required of advertising account executives, many employees work their way up through the company, from assistant to account executive to account manager and finally to department head. In smaller agencies, where promotions depend on experience and leadership, advancement may occur slowly. In larger firms, management training programs are often required for advancement. Continuing education is occasionally offered to account executives in these firms, often through local colleges or special seminars provided by professional societies.

EARNINGS

According to the U.S. Department of Labor, advertising account executives earned salaries that ranged from less than $22,390 to $92,800 or more annually in 2007, with median annual earnings of approximately $42,820. In smaller agencies, the salary may be much lower ($20,000 or less), and in larger firms, it is often much higher (over $150,000). Salary bonuses are common for account executives. Benefits typically include vacation and sick leave, health and life insurance, and a retirement plan.

WORK ENVIRONMENT

It is not uncommon for advertising account executives to work long hours, including evenings and weekends. Informal meetings with clients, for example, frequently take place after normal business hours. In addition, some travel may be required when clients are based in other cities or states or when account executives must attend industry conferences.

Advertising agencies are usually highly charged with energy and are both physically and psychologically exciting places to work. The account executive works with others as a team in a creative environment where a lot of ideas are exchanged among colleagues.

As deadlines are critical in advertising, it is important that account executives possess the ability to handle pressure and stress effectively. Patience and flexibility are also essential, as are organization and time management skills.

OUTLOOK

The growth of the advertising industry depends on the health of the economy. In a thriving economy, advertising budgets are large, consumers tend to respond to advertising campaigns, and new products and services that require promotion are increasingly developed. Although the economy has been weaker as of late, the U.S. Department of Labor still predicts that employment for advertising account executives will grow faster than the average for all occupations through 2016.

Opportunities for advertising account executives should be strong due to the growth of online advertising, cable television channels, and other advertising mediums. Growth will also occur as a result of the increasing Hispanic population in the United States. Advertisers are creating specialized advertising and marketing campaigns to reach this growing demographic.

Most opportunities for advertising account executives will be in larger cities, such as Chicago, New York, and Los Angeles, that enjoy a high concentration of businesses. Competition for these jobs, however, will be intense. The successful candidate will be a college graduate with a lot of creativity, strong communications skills, and extensive experience in the advertising industry. Those able to speak another language will have an edge because of the increasing supply of products and services offered in foreign markets.

FOR MORE INFORMATION

For profiles of advertising workers and career information, contact
Advertising Educational Foundation
220 East 42nd Street, Suite 3300
New York, NY 10017-5806
Tel: 212-986-8060
http://www.aef.com

The AAF combines the mutual interests of corporate advertisers, agencies, media companies, suppliers, and academia. Visit its Web site to learn more about internships, scholarships, and awards.

American Advertising Federation (AAF)
1101 Vermont Avenue, NW, Suite 500
Washington, DC 20005-6306
Tel: 800-999-2231
Email: aaf@aaf.org
http://www.aaf.org

For industry information, contact
American Association of Advertising Agencies
405 Lexington Avenue, 18th Floor
New York, NY 10174-1801
Tel: 212-682-2500
http://www.aaaa.org

For information on the practice, study, and teaching of marketing, contact
American Marketing Association
311 South Wacker Drive, Suite 5800
Chicago, IL 60606-6629
Tel: 800-262-1150
http://www.marketingpower.com

Antiques and Art Dealers

QUICK FACTS

School Subjects
Art
Art history
Business
Family and consumer science

Personal Skills
Artistic
Leadership/management

Work Environment
Primarily indoors
Primarily multiple locations

Minimum Education Level
High school diploma

Salary Range
$15,000 to $30,000 to $1 million

Certification or Licensing
None available

Outlook
About as fast as the average

DOT
N/A

GOE
N/A

NOC
0621

O*NET-SOC
N/A

OVERVIEW

Antiques and art dealers make a living acquiring, displaying, and selling antiques and art. By strict definition, antiques are often defined as items more than 100 years old. However, over the last two decades, the term "antique" has been applied to furniture, jewelry, clothing, art, household goods, and many other collectibles, dating back to as recently as the 1970s. People collect a wide array of items, from traditional paintings and sculptures to unique period toys and cigar boxes. Many antiques and art dealers are self-employed and go into business after discovering an interest in collecting pieces themselves. The Antiques and Collectibles National Association estimates there are approximately 200,000 to 250,000 antique dealers in the United States, based in antique shops, antique malls, and on the Internet.

HISTORY

Interest in collecting antiques and art can be traced back to the Renaissance, when people began to admire and prize Greek and Roman antiquities such as coins, manuscripts, sculptures, paintings, and pieces of architecture. In order to fulfill public interest and curiosity, as well as to supply the growing number of private and public collections, many pieces from Egypt, Italy, and Greece were looted and carried off to other countries.

The collectibles market, as it is known today, consists of everyday household objects, as well as furniture, clothing, art, and even automobiles, usually originating from another time period. After World War I, interest in collectibles grew. Many people began to purchase, preserve, and display pieces in their homes. As interest grew, so did the need for antiques and art businesses and dealers.

There are different categories of collectibles and different ways and reasons to acquire them. Some people choose to collect pieces from different time periods such as American Colonial or Victorian; others collect by the pattern or brand, such as Chippendale furniture or Coca-Cola memorabilia. Some people collect objects related to their career or business. For example, a physician may collect early surgical instruments, while a pharmacist may be interested in antique apothecary cabinets. A growing category in the collectibles industry is ephemera. Ephemera include theater programs, postcards, cigarette cards, and food labels, among others. These items were produced without lasting value or survival in mind. Though many pieces of ephemera can be purchased inexpensively, others, especially items among the first of their kind or in excellent condition, are rare and considered very valuable.

Some larger antiques and art dealers specialize and deal only with items from a particular time period or design. However, most dealers collect, buy, and sell all kinds of previously owned household items and decor. Such shops will carry items ranging from dining room furniture to jewelry to cooking molds.

The idea of what is worth collecting constantly changes with time and the public's tastes and interests. Art tastes range from traditional to contemporary, from Picasso to Warhol. Items representing the rock music industry of the 1960s and 1970s, as well as household items and furniture of the 1970s, are highly sought after today. Dealers not only stock their stores with items currently in demand but keep an eye on the collectibles of the future.

THE JOB

For Sandra Naujokas, proprietor of Favorite Things Antique Shop, in Orland Park, Illinois, the antiques business is never boring. More than 25 years ago, she started a collection of English-style china, and she's been hooked on antiques and collecting ever since. Naujokas spends her workday greeting customers and answering any questions they may have. When business slows down, she cleans the store and prices inventory. Sometimes people will bring in items for resale. It's up to Naujokas to carefully inspect each piece and settle on a price. She relies on pricing manuals such as *Kovels' Antiques & Collectibles Price List* and *Schroeder's Antiques Price*

Guide, which give guidelines and a suggested price on a wide range of items.

Naujokas also goes on a number of shopping expeditions each year to restock her store. Besides rummage sales and auctions, she relies on buying trips to different parts of the country and abroad to find regional items. At times, she is invited to a person's home to view items for sale. "It's important to be open to all possibilities," Naujokas says.

She also participates in several shows a year, in order to reach customers that normally would not travel to the store's location. "You need to do a variety of things to advertise your wares," Naujokas advises.

She also promotes her business by advertising in her town's travel brochure, the local newspapers, and by direct mail campaigns. Her schedule is grueling, as the store is open seven days a week, but Naujokas enjoys the work and the challenge of being an antiques dealer. Besides the social aspect—interacting with all sorts of people and situations—Naujokas loves having the first choice of items for her personal collections. Her advice for people interested in having their own antique store, "You have to really like the items you intend to sell."

REQUIREMENTS

High School

You can become an antiques or art dealer with a high school diploma, though many successful dealers have become specialists in their field partly through further education. While in high school, concentrate on history and art classes to familiarize yourself with the particular significance and details of different periods in time and the corresponding art of the period. Consider studying home economics if you plan to specialize in household items. This knowledge can come in handy when distinguishing a wooden rolling pin from a wooden butter paddle, for example.

English and speech classes to improve communication skills are also helpful. Antiques and art dealing is a people-oriented business. For this reason, it's crucial to be able to deal efficiently with different types of people and situations. Operating your own small business will also require skills such as accounting, simple bookkeeping, and marketing, so business classes are recommended.

Postsecondary Training

While a college education is not required, a degree in fine arts, art history, or history will give you a working knowledge of the antiques you sell and the historical periods from which they originated. Another option is obtaining a degree in business or entrepreneurship. Such knowledge will help you to run a successful business.

Certification or Licensing
Presently, there are no certification programs available for antiques dealers. However, if you plan to open your own antique store, you will need a local business license or permit.

In addition, if you wish to conduct appraisals, it will be necessary to take appraisal courses that are appropriate for your interest or antique specialty. Certification is not required of those interested in working as an appraiser, but it is highly recommended, according to the International Society of Appraisers (ISA)—which administers an accreditation and certification program to its members. Obtaining accreditation or certification will demonstrate your knowledge and expertise in appraisal and attract customers. To obtain accreditation, candidates must have three years of experience in appraising, complete the ISA Core Course in Appraisal Studies, and pass an examination. In order to become certified, individuals must complete additional training in their specialty area, submit two appraisals for peer review, complete professional development study, and pass a comprehensive examination.

Other Requirements
To be an antiques or art dealer, you'll need patience—and lots of it. Keeping your store well stocked with antiques, art, or other collectibles takes numerous buying trips to auctions, estate sales, flea markets, rummage sales, and even to foreign countries. Many times you'll have to sort through boxes of ordinary "stuff" before coming across a treasure. Unless you're lucky enough to have a large staff, you will have to make these outings by yourself. However, most dealers go into the profession because they enjoy the challenge of hunting for valuable pieces.

In addition to being patient in the hunt for treasure, art dealers also have to be patient when dealing with clients. Works of art can cost thousands, even millions of dollars; as a result, purchases are typically not quick decisions. The ability to work with a client over some time and gradually persuade them to invest in a piece takes time, skill, patience and tact.

Tact is another must-have quality for success in this industry. Remember the old adage—one person's trash is another person's treasure.

Finally, with the growth of online auction sites such as eBay, computer skills have come to be an essential part of the antiques or collectibles dealer's toolkit.

EXPLORING

To explore this field further, you may want to start by visiting an antique store or art gallery. If you see valuable treasures as opposed to dull paintings, old furniture, outdated books, or dusty collectibles, then chances are this is the job for you.

You can also tune to an episode of public television's traveling antiques show, *Antiques Roadshow* (http://www.pbs.org/wgbh/pages/roadshow), where people are encouraged to bring family treasures or rummage sale bargains for appraisal by antiques industry experts.

EMPLOYERS

Many antiques and art dealers and are self-employed, operating their own shops or renting space at a local mall. Others operate solely through traveling art shows or through mail-order catalogues. Some dealers prefer to work as employees of larger antique or art galleries. In general, the more well known the dealer, the more permanent and steady the business. Prestigious auction houses such as Christie's or Sotheby's are attractive places to work, but competition for such jobs is fierce.

STARTING OUT

All dealers have a great interest in antiques or art and are collectors themselves. Often, their businesses result from an overabundance of their personal collections. There are many ways to build your collection and create inventory worthy of an antiques business. Attending yard sales is an inexpensive way to build your inventory; you'll never know what kind of valuables you will come across. Flea markets, local art galleries, and antique malls will provide great purchasing opportunities and give you the chance to check out the competition. Sandra Naujokas finds that spring is an especially busy time for collecting. As people do their "spring cleaning," many decide to part with household items and décor they no longer want or need.

ADVANCEMENT

For those working out of their homes or renting showcase space at malls or larger shops, advancement in this field can mean opening your own antique shop or art gallery. Besides a business license, dealers that open their own stores need to apply for a seller's permit and a state tax identification number.

At this point, advancement is based on the success of the business. To ensure that their business thrives and expands, dealers need to develop advertising and marketing ideas to keep their business in the public's eye. Besides using the local library or Internet for ideas on opening their own businesses, newer dealers often turn to people who are already in the antiques and art business for valuable advice.

EARNINGS

It is difficult to gauge what antiques and art dealers earn because of the vastness of the industry. Some internationally known, high-end antique stores and art galleries dealing with many pieces of priceless furniture or works of art may make millions of dollars in yearly profits. This, however, is the exception. It is impossible to compare the high-end dealer with the lower end market. The majority of antiques and art dealers are comparatively small in size and type of inventory. Some dealers work only part time or rent showcase space from established shops.

According to a survey conducted by the Antiques and Collectibles National Association, the average showcase dealer earns about $1,000 a month in gross profits. From there, each dealer earns a net profit as determined by the piece or pieces sold, after overhead and other business costs. Note that annual earnings vary greatly for antiques and art dealers due to factors such as size and specialization of the store, location, the market, and current trends and tastes of the public.

WORK ENVIRONMENT

Much of antiques and art dealers' time is spent indoors. Many smaller antique shops and art galleries do not operate with a large staff, so dealers must be prepared to work alone at times. Also, there may be large gaps of time between customers. Most stores are open at least five days a week and operate during regular business hours, though some have extended shopping hours in the evening.

However, dealers are not always stuck in their store. Buying trips and shopping expeditions give them opportunities to restock their inventory, not to mention explore different regions of the country or world. Naujokas finds that spring is the busiest time for building her store's merchandise, while the holiday season is a busy selling time.

OUTLOOK

According to the Antiques and Collectibles National Association (ACNA), the collectibles industry should enjoy moderate growth in future years. The Internet has quickly become a popular way to buy and sell antiques and art. Though this medium has introduced collecting to many people worldwide, it has also had an adverse affect on the industry, namely for dealers and businesses that sell antiques and art in more traditional settings such as a shop or mall, or at a trade show. However, some industry experts predict that the popularity of Web sites devoted to selling collectibles will level off. There is a great social aspect to collecting art and antiques. They believe that people want to see, feel, and touch the items they are interested in purchasing, which is obviously not possible to do while surfing the Web.

Though the number of authentic antique art and collectibles—items more than 100 years old—is limited, new items will be in vogue as collectibles. Also, people will be ready to sell old furniture and other belongings to make room for new, modern purchases. It is unlikely that there will ever be a shortage of inventory worthy of an antique shop or art gallery.

FOR MORE INFORMATION

For industry information, antique show schedules, and appraisal information, contact
    Antiques and Collectibles National Association
    PO Box 4389
    Davidson, NC 28036-4389
    Tel: 800-287-7127
    http://www.antiqueandcollectible.com

For art resources and listings of galleries, contact
    Art Dealers Association of America
    205 Lexington Avenue, Suite 901
    New York, NY 10016-6022
    Tel: 212-488-5550
    http://www.artdealers.org

Contact the FADA for information on art galleries nationwide and special events.
    Fine Art Dealers Association (FADA)
    PO Box D1
    Carmel, CA 93921-0729
    http://www.fada.com

For information about appraising and certification, contact
    International Society of Appraisers
    230 East Ohio Street, Suite 400

Chicago, IL 60611-3645
Tel: 312-224-2567
Email: isa@isa-appraisers.org
http://www.isa-appraisers.org

For programming schedules and tour information on the public television show that highlights unique and sometimes priceless antique finds, visit
Antiques Roadshow
http://www.pbs.org/wgbh/pages/roadshow

For information on collecting, art and antique shows, and collecting clubs, visit
Collectors.org
http://www.collectors.org

Auctioneers

QUICK FACTS

School Subjects
Art
Mathematics
Speech

Personal Skills
Helping/teaching
Leadership/management

Work Environment
Indoors and outdoors
Primarily multiple locations

Minimum Education Level
High school diploma

Salary Range
$10,000 to $50,000 to $100,000

Certification or Licensing
Recommended (certification)
Required by certain states (licensing)

Outlook
About as fast as the average

DOT
294

GOE
N/A

NOC
6411

O*NET-SOC
41-9099.00

OVERVIEW

Auctioneers appraise, assemble, and advertise goods, which they subsequently sell to the highest bidder during an auction. They act as salespeople for the family, company, agency, or nonprofit organization selling the items to be auctioned. Depending on their area of expertise, they may auction off anything from a rare book to an entire office building.

HISTORY

In the United States many of the oldest auction firms are located in cities on the East Coast. For instance, Christie's in New York City is famous for auctioning luxury items such as fine art and celebrity memorabilia. Auctions have also long been popular in rural areas. Prior to the development of department stores, rural families had their own methods of dispensing with and acquiring the items and machinery they needed. For small or individual items, a barter or trade sometimes was made to exchange a needed tool or other possession. When many different items were being sold, however, a family would hold an auction, and an auctioneer would be hired to assist the family in disposing of the property. Families sometimes held auctions to raise cash or because they were moving and could not take along all their possessions.

Auctions are a popular way to buy farm equipment, real estate, artwork, livestock, or personal property from estates. An auction disposes of many varied items fairly quickly by selling one item to the highest bidder and then immediately moving through the rest of the collection. Auctions also are a popular way to raise money for charities and other groups. They are fun as well as functional and have become increasingly common in both rural areas and cities.

THE JOB

An auctioneer's work has two main facets: the preliminary preparation and evaluation and the selling itself. The former takes more time and skill and is less familiar to most people. Prior to the auction itself, the auctioneer meets with the sellers to review the property to be sold. The auctioneer makes note of the lowest bid, called the "reserved bid," that the sellers will accept for each item. The auctioneer also advises clients when an item should be sold "absolute," or without a minimum bid. If there are legal issues to be discussed, an auctioneer confers with the sellers.

The most time-consuming activity often is the appraisal of the goods. The auctioneer determines the value of each item and compares it to the reserve bid established by the sellers. The auctioneer makes notes on the type of item being sold, its history, and any unique qualities the item may have. This background information can encourage higher bids and increase buyer interest.

Once the appraisal has taken place, an auctioneer must organize the items in the area where the auction is to be held. Sometimes the auctioneer issues a catalog or booklet describing the items for sale for that particular day. The catalog also may list the sequence in which the items will be sold so buyers know when the items they want will be up for sale. In addition to the catalog, auctioneers organize any advertising needed to promote the sale. Newspaper and magazine ads, emails, flyers, signs, and broadcast announcements can reach people from many different areas and bring in a large crowd. Some rural areas hold auctions as special attractions for tourists around summer holidays or to commemorate town events and local celebrations.

Usually the auctioneer organizes and sets up the auction far enough in advance for people to come early, peruse the area, and see what is of interest to them. Antique furniture and clothing, farm equipment, and artwork are some of the things sold at auctions. Other auctions concentrate on large industrial machinery or cars, as well as livestock, stamps, coins, and books.

The auctioneer works to help both the buyer and the seller. An auctioneer is familiar enough with the potential value of the items and begins bids at a certain price. The encouragement and stimulation an auctioneer provides, however, often is matched by the excitement and competition among the buyers. Auctioneers must be

An auctioneer wields his gavel as more than 300 foreclosed homes are auctioned to the highest bidder. *(Jim West, The Image Works)*

quick-thinking and comfortable addressing crowds, not only offering them information about the items for sale but at times acting as entertainers to keep the crowd interested.

Auctioneers coordinate the pace of the auction and judge which items should be sold first. Sometimes to boost people's interest, an auctioneer saves the most popular items for last. At other times the best articles are sold first so that those who weren't able to purchase their first choice will feel free to bid on other items.

Auctioneers commonly enlist the help of assistants, who carry items to the auctioneer, ensuring a steady flow of goods. In addition, another assistant may be in charge of collecting money, issuing receipts, and keeping track of the purchaser of each item.

Most auctions follow a typical pattern. The items for sale are made available for inspection in a catalog or a display. In the case of real estate auctions, however, photographs may be circulated. In some instances, land that is miles away can be sold, though the auctioneer will describe some history and features of the area. Often these types of auctions take less time, but the preparation is more detailed. Auctioneers must know the dimensions of the buildings they are selling, boundary lines for lots and farms, and whether any money is owed or any environmental hazard exists on the property, as well as information about the terms of payment and zoning laws.

Randy Wells is the president of the National Auctioneers Association, the leading professional organization for auctioneers. He lives in Post Falls, Idaho, but has conducted auctions throughout the United States—from Anchorage, Alaska, to San Diego, California, and from Portland, Oregon, to Portland, Maine. He has been an auctioneer since 1985 and conducts personal property, benefit, and real estate auctions. "I entered this career totally by accident," he says. "My wife and I purchased a local auction business to supplement another business that we owned. The auction business grew and we ended up selling our other businesses—mainly because my wife and I really enjoy the auction business. It has been very good to us and our family. Because of the auction business we were able to send both of our children to college. Our daughter lives in Portland, Oregon, and owns her own auction business. She is very busy and specializes in benefit auctions. Her Web site is http://www.benefitauctions360.com and she is a past International Auctioneer Champion, so we are truly an auction family."

REQUIREMENTS

High School
A high school diploma generally is a basic requirement for auctioneers. Classes in sales, mathematics, speech, art, art history, and economics are useful.

Postsecondary Training
Training for auctioneers is available at many schools across the country. For a list of schools and programs, visit http://www.auctioneers.org/web/2007/06/education.aspx. The National Auctioneers Association (NAA) offers online courses for auctioneers in topics such as ethics, introduction to advertising, and care of the voice. The NAA Education Institute offers the Certified Auctioneers Institute profession program, taught at Indiana University in Bloomington. Some aspiring auctioneers also learn the trade by apprenticing with experienced auctioneers.

Auctioneer training can involve appraising and item presentation, as well as speech classes so that auctioneers do not strain their voices while working long hours. Auctioneers who plan to concentrate on specific areas may take classes to supplement their training. Livestock and real estate auctions require specialized knowledge. In addition, some auctioneers have backgrounds in art or antiques.

Auctioneers must be effective speakers. Their job is to command attention and interest in the items through the power of their voice and their personal manner and good humor. Auctioneers should have a great deal of stamina, since auctions often take place outdoors in warm weather and can last for many hours at a stretch. Auctioneers must also be alert so they can keep track of the crowd activity, the progress of the assistants, and the selling of the goods.

Because of all the deliberation that goes into preparing an auction, an auctioneer should like working with people. A keen sense of evaluation and an honest nature also are useful attributes.

Certification or Licensing
Because they handle large sums of money, most auctioneers are bonded; however, licensing for auctioneers varies from state to state. Approximately 27 states require auctioneers to be licensed. Licensing requirements vary, so be sure to contact the licensing board for the state in which you would like to work for more information.

The NAA Education Institute offers the following professional designation programs to practicing auctioneers who meet its experiential, educational, and ethical standards: Certified Auctioneers Institute, auction technology specialist, benefit auctioneer specialist, certified estate specialist, accredited auctioneer real estate, graduate personal property appraiser, and graduate personal property appraiser-master. "Each one will help you become a better and more professional auctioneer," says Randy Wells.

Other Requirements
Wells says that to be successful in this career, you need "people skills and communication skills." He also says, "Auctioneers need to have the capabilities to deal with bankers, attorneys, estate planners, real estate professionals, CPA's, and many other professionals."

Auctioneers who work in specialized areas, such as real estate and livestock, must conform to additional regulations. Those who sell land must be licensed real estate sales agents or brokers. Auctioneers should be familiar with laws and regulations in the states in which they practice.

EXPLORING

Randy Wells recommends that aspiring auctioneers "go to an accredited auction school. Join your state association, the National Auctioneers Association, local civic clubs, and your local Chamber of Commerce. You will learn that you will gain a lot both personally and professionally by being involved in your community and your industry associations through networking with other business associates."

You can also explore this field by attending an auction to see firsthand the responsibilities that are involved. Classes in speech, drama, and communications may be helpful because auctioneers rely heavily on their voices, not only for speaking and presentation but also to get the buyer's attention through style and performance.

More direct involvement is possible as well. Charities and other social organizations occasionally use nonprofessionals for fundraising auctions, and established auctioneers often hire part-time assistants. It may also be useful to read periodicals, such as *Auctioneer* (published by the National Auctioneers Association), that publish articles about the field.

EMPLOYERS

Auctioneers often work as consultants on a freelance basis. They may be hired by private individuals or large companies anywhere that goods are offered for sale to the highest bidder. Others may work for private auction houses, which usually are located in large metropolitan areas such as New York, Los Angeles, and Chicago, as well as smaller cities. Those who wish to focus on specific areas such as real estate, art, or farm equipment should, of course, seek consulting assignments or permanent positions in locations and/or with companies where these items are sold; for example, farm equipment generally is auctioned in rural areas.

STARTING OUT

Beginning auctioneers may work as assistants, handling money and receipts or presenting the sale items to the experienced auctioneer. They also may begin by working at local and county fairs or smaller auctions.

Professional trade schools may offer placement services or internships that link beginners with established practitioners. Beginners may have to work part time until they gain experience and become better known. Auctioneers who work for large auction houses may receive more assignments as they become more experienced and complete training offered by the firm.

ADVANCEMENT

Professional auctioneers must have a reputation for skilled and honest performance. Since most auctioneers get paid by commission, they may decide to specialize in selling real estate, farm equipment,

Percentage of Sales by Auction Specialty, 2003-06

Automobiles:	37.8 percent
Land and Agricultural Real Estate:	10.3 percent
Agricultural Machinery and Equipment:	8.3 percent
Livestock:	7.9 percent
Charity:	6.7 percent
Residential Real Estate:	6.3 percent
Commercial and Industrial Real Estate:	6.2 percent
Art, Antiques, and Collectibles:	5.6 percent
Commercial and Industrial Machinery and Equipment:	5.4 percent
Personal Property:	4.5 percent
Other:	1.0 percent
Intellectual Property:	0.1 percent

Source: National Auctioneers Association

or artwork—areas that are likely to bring in more revenue for less preparation and shorter presentations.

Auctioneers who work with auction houses may move up the ranks and obtain more prestigious assignments. Auctioneers also advance as they develop their knowledge in specialized areas. Some people move into different lines of work but keep auctioning as a side job.

EARNINGS

Part-time auctioneers earn close to $10,000, while full-time auctioneers typically earn more than $20,000. The best-paid auctioneers earn $50,000 to $100,000 or more. On a daily basis, pay ranges between $100 and $2,000.

Auctioneers usually are paid on commission. Part-time auctioneers sometimes supplement their income by assisting more experienced workers, acting as cashiers, assisting with publicity, or helping to organize the items.

Auctioneers who work for a company usually receive benefits such as vacation days, sick leave, health and life insurance, and a savings and pension program. Self-employed auctioneers must provide their own benefits.

WORK ENVIRONMENT

Because auctioneers often travel to an assignment, they may encounter a wide range of working conditions. Auctions are held year-round. They take place in cities and small towns and occur in all types of weather. Auctioneers may work inside in a large hall or outside during a state fair. The type of goods being sold may also dictate their working conditions; for instance, farm equipment is commonly sold outdoors on the site of the owner's farm.

"My work environment changes constantly," says Randy Wells, "depending on which state or type of auction we are working in. I not only do benefit auctions and real estate auctions, but I also give several different business seminars and teach other auctioneers how to do what we do. In this day and age, we are living in a global economy, so the auction industry relies heavily upon technology. I spend a lot of time on the Internet communicating with clients and doing market research.

Auctioneers often are provided with a podium and a microphone, which are especially important at large auctions, which can draw more than 2,000 people. This allows the auctioneer to keep the crowd's attention when the noise and activity level become distracting or stressful.

OUTLOOK

The outlook for auctioneers is good, especially for those who have developed a specialty, such as real estate. Auctioneers with polished skills and a strong delivery usually have little trouble finding work. For an ambitious auctioneer who is willing to travel to various locations and invest time to gain experience, regular employment is possible, either as an independent auctioneer or as a staff member of an auction firm.

"Auctioneers will always be needed, but the playing field is changing," says Randy Wells. "Be involved in your industry via the aforementioned associations and continuing education opportunities and you will know about change before it affects you. This is not an easy business to get into, but if you opt to become an auctioneer, it is a profession you will enjoy every single day. Online auctions conducted over the Internet are growing at a very high rate and this may have an effect on auctioneers conducting live auctions."

Many auctioneers get assignments based on their reputation and notoriety within an area. Thus, auctioneers may find it difficult to re-establish themselves if they move to another area. Also, some types of auctions are found only in certain areas. Art auctions, for example, generally take place in cities, while livestock, farm equipment, and farmland most often are sold in rural areas.

FOR MORE INFORMATION

Contact the following organization for career and educational information:

National Auctioneers Association
8880 Ballentine Street
Overland Park, KS 66214-1900
Tel: 913-541-8084
Email: info@auctioneers.org
http://www.auctioneers.org

Automobile Sales Workers

OVERVIEW

Automobile sales workers inform customers about new or used automobiles, and they prepare payment, financing, and insurance papers for customers who have purchased a vehicle. It is their job to persuade the customer that the product they are selling is the best choice. They prospect new customers by mail, by telephone, or through personal contacts. To stay informed about their products, sales workers regularly attend training sessions about the vehicles they sell. There are approximately 280,000 automobile sales workers employed in the United States.

HISTORY

By the 1920s, nearly 20,000 automobile dealerships dotted the American landscape as the "Big Three" automobile makers—Ford, General Motors, and Chrysler—increased production every year to meet the public's growing demand for automobiles. Automobile sales workers began to earn higher and higher wages. As automobiles became more popular, the need for an organization to represent the growing industry became evident. In 1917, the National Automobile Dealers Association (NADA) was founded to change the way Congress viewed automobiles. In the early years, NADA worked to convince Congress that cars weren't a luxury item, as they had been classified, but vital to the economy. The group prevented the government from converting all automotive factories to wartime work during World War I and reduced a proposed luxury tax on automobiles from 5 percent to 3 percent.

QUICK FACTS

School Subjects
Business
Speech

Personal Skills
Communication/ideas
Helping/teaching

Work Environment
Primarily indoors
Primarily one location

Minimum Education Level
High school diploma

Salary Range
$20,000 to $44,770 to $92,000

Certification or Licensing
Voluntary

Outlook
About as fast as the average

DOT
273

GOE
10.03.01

NOC
6421

O*NET-SOC
11-2022.00

During the lean years of the Depression in the early 1930s, automobile sales fell sharply until President Franklin Delano Roosevelt's New Deal helped jumpstart the industry. Roosevelt signed the Code of Fair Competition for the Motor Vehicle Retailing Trade, which established standards in the automotive manufacturing and sales industries. By 1942, the number of dealerships in the United States more than doubled to 44,000.

Automobile sales workers have suffered an image problem for much of the career's history. Customers sometimes felt that they were pressured to purchase new cars at unfair prices and that the dealer's profit was too large. The 1958 Price Labeling Law, which mandated cars display window stickers listing manufacturer suggested retail prices and other information, helped ease relations between sales workers and their customers. However, in the fiercely competitive automobile market, sales workers' selling methods and the thrifty customer remained at odds.

When it came to used vehicles, there was no way for customers to know whether they were getting a fair deal. Even in the automobile's early history, used vehicles have been popular. From 1919 through the 1950s, used car sales consistently exceeded new car sales. Despite the popularity of used vehicles, the automobile sales industry didn't quite know how to handle them. Some dealers lost money on trade-ins when they stayed on the lot too long. After debating for years how to handle trade-ins, dealers finally began today's common practice of applying their value toward down payments on new cars.

The industry suffered personnel shortages when the armed forces recruited mechanics during World War II. This affected the service departments of dealerships, which traditionally have generated the biggest profits, and many dealers had to be creative to stay in business. During these lean times, sales gimmicks, such as giveaways and contests, came into increased use. According to a history of NADA, one Indiana dealer bought radios, refrigerators, freezers, and furnaces to sell in his showroom and sold toys at Christmas to stay in business.

The energy crisis of the 1970s brought hard times to the entire automotive industry. Many dealerships were forced to close, and those that survived made little profit. In 1979 alone, 600 dealerships closed. As of 2006, according to NADA, there were 21,200 dealerships nationwide (down from 47,500 in 1951) accounting for about 14 percent of all retail sales and employing more than 1.2 million people. Most dealerships today sell more makes of cars than dealerships of the past. Still, they face competition from newer forms of automobile retailers, such as automotive superstores, the automotive equivalent to discount stores like Wal-Mart. Also, automotive information is becoming more widely available on the Internet, eroding the consumer's need for automobile sales workers as a source of information about automobiles.

THE JOB

The automobile sales worker's main task is to sell. Today, many dealerships try to soften the image of salesmen and women by emphasizing no pressure, even one-price shopping. But automobile dealers expect their employees to sell, and selling in most cases involves some degree of persuasion. The automobile sales worker informs customers of everything there is to know about a particular vehicle. A good sales worker finds out what the customer wants or needs and suggests automobiles that may fit that need—empowering the customer with choice and a feeling that he or she is getting a fair deal.

Since the sticker price on new cars is only a starting point to be bargained down, and since many customers come to dealerships already knowing which car they would like to buy, sales workers spend much of their time negotiating the final selling price.

Most dealerships have special sales forces for new cars, used cars, trucks, recreational vehicles, and leasing operations. In each specialty, sales workers learn all aspects of the product they must sell. They may attend information and training seminars sponsored by manufacturers. New car sales workers, especially, are constantly learning new car features. Sales workers inform customers about a car's performance, fuel economy, safety features, and luxuries or accessories. They are able to talk about innovations over previous models, engine and mechanical specifications, ease of handling, and ergonomic designs. Good sales workers also keep track of competing models' features.

In many ways, used car sales workers have a more daunting mass of information to keep track of. Whereas new car sales workers concentrate on the most current features of an automobile, used car sales workers must keep track of all features from several model years. Good used car dealers can look at a car and note immediately the make, model, and year of a car. Because of popular two- and three-year leasing options, the used car market has increased by nearly 50 percent in the last 10 years.

Successful sales workers are generally good readers of a person's character. They can determine exactly what it is a customer is looking for in a new car. They must be friendly and understanding of customers' needs in order to put them at ease (due to the amount of money involved, car buying is an unpleasant task for most people). They are careful not to oversell the car by providing the customers with information they may not care about or understand, thus confusing them. For example, if a customer only cares about style, sales workers will not impress upon him all of the wonderful intricacies of a new high-tech engine design.

Sales workers greet customers and ask if they have any questions about a particular model. It's very important for sales workers to have immediate and confident answers to all questions about the vehicles they're selling. When a sale is difficult, they occasionally use psychological methods, or subtle "prodding," to influence customers. Some sales workers use aggressive selling methods and pressure the customer to purchase the car. Although recent trends are turning away from the pressure-sell, competition will keep these types of selling methods prevalent in the industry, albeit at a slightly toned-down level.

Customers usually make more than one visit to a dealership before purchasing a new or used car. Because one sales worker "works" the customer on the first visit—forming an acquaintanceship and learning the customer's personality—he or she will usually stay with that customer until the sale is made or lost. The sales worker usually schedules times for the customer to come in and talk more about the car in order to stay with the customer through the process and not lose the sale to another sales worker. Sales workers may make follow-up phone calls to make special offers or remind customers of certain features that make a particular model better than the competition, or they may send mailings for the same purpose.

In addition to providing the customer with information about the car, sales workers discuss financing packages, leasing options, and warranty. When the sale is made, they go over the contract with the customer and obtain a signature. Frequently the exact model with all of the features the customer requested is not in the dealership, and the sales worker must place an order with the manufacturer or distributor. When purchasing a new or used vehicle, many customers trade in their old vehicle. Sales workers appraise the trade-in and offer a price.

At some dealerships sales workers also do public relations and marketing work. They establish promotions to get customers into their showrooms, print fliers to distribute in the local community, and make television or radio advertisements. In order to keep their name in the back (or front) of the customer's mind, they may send past customers birthday and holiday cards or similar "courtesies." Most of the larger dealerships also have an auto maintenance and repair service department. Sales workers may help customers establish a periodic maintenance schedule or suggest repair work.

Computers are used at a growing number of dealerships. Customers use computers to answer questions they may have, consult price indexes, check on ready availability of parts, and even compare the car they're interested in with the competition's equivalent. Although

A sales worker and customer review a sales brochure at a car dealership. (Willie Hill Jr., The Image Works)

computers can't replace human interaction and sell the car to customers who need reassurances, they do help the customer feel more informed and more in control when buying a car.

Internet sales specialists are sales workers who specialize in selling vehicles at a dealership's Web site. They manage Internet sales leads and answer the questions of customers. They work with Webmasters to keep the dealership's Web site up to date and attractive to potential buyers. Internet sales specialists help develop special Web-only sales and promotions and ensure that the latest and most comprehensive information is posted at the Web site. They also arrange test drives and schedule deliveries of vehicles that have been purchased by customers on the Web.

REQUIREMENTS

High School
Because thorough knowledge of automobiles—from how they work to how they drive and how they are manufactured—is essential for a successful sales worker, automotive maintenance classes in high school are an excellent place to begin. Classes in English, speech, drama, and psychology will help you to achieve the excellent speaking skills you will need to make a good sale and gain customer confidence and respect. Classes in business and mathematics will teach you to manage and prioritize your workload, prepare goals, and work

confidently with customer financing packages. As computers become increasingly prevalent in every aspect of the industry, you should take as many computer classes as you can. Speaking a second language will give you an advantage, especially in major cities with large minority populations.

Postsecondary Training
Those who seek management-level positions will have a distinct advantage if they possess a college degree, preferably in business or marketing, but other degrees, whether they be in English, economics, or psychology, are no less important, so long as applicants have good management skills and can sell cars. Many schools offer degrees in automotive marketing and automotive aftermarket management that prepare students to take high-level management positions. Even with a two- or four-year degree in hand, many dealerships may not begin new hires directly as managers, but first start them out as sales workers.

Certification or Licensing
By completing the certified automotive merchandiser program offered by the NADA, students seeking entry-level positions gain a significant advantage. Certification assures employers that workers have the basic skills they require.

Other Requirements
In today's competitive job market you will need a high school diploma to land a job that offers growth possibilities, a good salary, and challenges; this includes jobs in the automobile sales industry. Employers prefer to hire entry-level employees who have had some previous experience in automotive services or in retail sales. They look for candidates who have good verbal, business, mathematics, electronics, and computer skills. A number of automotive sales and services courses and degrees are offered today at community colleges, vocational schools, independent organizations, and manufacturers. Sales workers should possess a valid driver's license and have a good driving record.

Sales workers must be enthusiastic, well-organized self-starters who thrive in a competitive environment. They must show excitement and authority about each type of car they sell and convince customers, without being too pushy (though some pressure on the customer usually helps make the sale), that the car they're interested in is the "right" car, at the fairest price. Sales workers must be able to read a customer's personality and know when to be outgoing and when to pull back and be more reserved. A neat, professional appearance is also very important for sales workers.

EXPLORING

Automobile trade magazines and books, in addition to selling technique and business books, are excellent sources of information for someone considering a career in this field. Local and state automobile and truck dealer associations can also provide you with information on career possibilities in automobile and truck sales. Your local Yellow Pages have a listing under "associations" for dealer organizations in your area.

Students interested in automobile sales work might first stop by their local dealer and ask about training programs and job requirements there. On a busy day at any dealership there will be several sales workers on the floor selling cars. Students can witness the basic selling process by going to dealerships and unobtrusively watching and listening as sales workers talk with customers. Many dealerships hire students part time to wash and clean cars. This is a good way to see the types of challenges and pressures automobile sales workers experience every day. Although it may take a special kind of sales skill or a different approach to selling a $25,000 vehicle over $50 shoes, any type of retail sales job that requires frequent interaction with customers will prepare students for work as an automobile sales worker.

EMPLOYERS

Approximately 280,000 automobile sales workers are employed in the United States. Franchised automobile dealerships employ the majority of automobile sales workers in the United States. A franchised automobile dealer is a dealer that is formally recognized and authorized by the manufacturer to sell its vehicles. A small number of sales workers are employed by used car dealerships that are strictly independent and not recognized by any manufacturer. Automotive superstores need automobile sales workers as well, although some may argue that these workers aren't truly automobile sales specialists because they tend to have less training and experience in the automotive area.

STARTING OUT

Generally, those just out of high school are not going to land a job as an automobile sales worker; older customers do not feel comfortable making such a large investment through a teenager. Employers prefer to see some previous automotive service experience with certification, such as National Institute of Automotive Service Excellence certification, or postsecondary training in automotive selling, such as NADA's CAM program. Dealerships will hire those with proven sales skill in a different field for sales worker positions and give them on-the-job training.

Employers frequently post job openings at schools that provide postsecondary education in business administration or automotive marketing. Certified automotive technicians or body repairers who think they might eventually like to break into a sales job should look for employment at dealership service centers. They will have frequent contact with sales workers and make connections with dealership managers and owners, as well as become so familiar with one or more models of a manufacturer's cars that they will make well-informed, knowledgeable sales workers. You can also visit http://www.showroomtoday.com for job listings and advice on career development.

Some dealerships will hire young workers with little experience in automobile services but who can demonstrate proven skills in sales and a willingness to learn. These workers will learn on the job. They may first be given administrative tasks. Eventually they will accompany experienced sales workers on the showroom floor and learn "hands-on." After about a year, the workers will sell on their own, and managers will evaluate their selling skills in sales meetings and suggest ways they can improve their sales records.

ADVANCEMENT

The longer sales workers stay with a dealership, the larger their client base grows and the more cars are sold. Advancement for many sales workers comes in the form of increased earnings and customer loyalty. Other sales workers may be promoted through a combination of experience and further training or certification.

As positions open, sales workers with proven management skills go on to become assistant and general managers. Managers with excellent sales skills and a good client base may open a new franchise dealership or their own independent dealership.

The Society of Automotive Sales Professionals (SASP), a division of NADA, provides sales workers with advancement possibilities. Once sales workers have completed a certification process and have a minimum of six months' sales experience, they are eligible to participate in SASP seminars that stress improving the new car buying process by polishing a sales worker's professional image.

EARNINGS

Earnings for automobile sales workers vary depending on location, size, and method of salary. Previously, most dealerships paid their sales workers either straight commission or salary plus commission. This forced sales workers to become extremely aggressive in their selling strategy—and often too aggressive for many customers. With a new trend toward pressure-free selling, more sales workers are earning a straight salary. Many dealerships still offer incentives such as bonuses and profit sharing to encourage sales. The average hourly wage for automotive sales workers was $21.52 in 2007, according to the U.S. Department of Labor. This makes for an annual salary of approximately $44,770 a year. Those who work on a straight commission basis can earn more; however, their earnings are minimal during slow periods. Sales workers who are just getting started in the field may earn lower annual salaries for a few years as they work to establish a client base. They may start in the low $20,000s. According to Automotive Retailing Today, a coalition of all major automobile manufacturers and dealer organizations, automobile sales workers earn salaries that range from $30,000 to $92,000.

Benefits vary by dealership but often include health insurance and a paid vacation. An increasing number of employers will pay all or most of an employee's certification training.

WORK ENVIRONMENT

Sales workers for new car dealerships work in pleasant indoor showrooms. Most used car dealerships keep the majority of their cars in outdoor lots where sales workers may spend much of their day. Upon final arrangements for a sale, they work in comfortable office spaces at a desk. Suits are the standard attire. During slow periods, when competition among dealers is fierce, sales workers often work under pressure. They must not allow "lost" sales to discourage their work. The typical workweek is between 40 and 50 hours, although if business is good, a sales worker will work more. Since most customers shop for cars on the weekends and in the evenings, work hours are irregular.

OUTLOOK

Automobile dealerships are one of the businesses most severely affected by economic recession. Conversely, when the economy is strong, the automobile sales industry tends to benefit. For the sales worker, growth, in any percentage, is good news, as they are the so-called front-line professionals in the industry who are responsible for representing the dealerships and manufacturers and for getting their cars out on the streets. In the late 1990s and early 2000s, automobile sales were especially strong in the United States; however, a weak economy in recent years has caused some setbacks.

The automobile sales worker faces many future challenges. A shift in customer buying preferences and experience is forcing sales workers to re-evaluate their selling methods. Information readily available on the Internet helps customers shop for the most competitive financing or leasing package and read reviews on car and truck models that interest them. Transactions are still brokered at the dealership, but once consumers become more familiar with the Internet, many will shop and buy exclusively from home.

Another trend threatening dealers is automotive superstores, such as CarMax and AutoNation, where customers have a large inventory to select from at a base price and get information and ask questions about a car not from a sales worker, but from a computer. Sales workers are still needed to finalize the sale, but their traditional role at the dealership is lessened.

Nonetheless, the number of cars and trucks on U.S. roads is expected to increase, and opportunities in this lucrative, but stressful, career should continue to increase about as fast as the average.

FOR MORE INFORMATION

For industry information, contact
American International Automobile Dealers
211 North Union Street, Suite 300
Alexandria, VA 22314-2643
Tel: 800-462-4232
http://www.aiada.org

For information on accreditation and testing, contact
National Automobile Dealers Association
8400 Westpark Drive
McLean, VA 22102-5116
Tel: 800-252-6232
Email: nadainfo@nada.org
http://www.nada.org

For information on certification, contact
National Institute for Automotive Service Excellence
101 Blue Seal Drive, SE, Suite 101
Leesburg, VA 20175-5646
Tel: 703-669-6600
http://www.asecert.org

For information on careers, visit
Automotive Careers Today
http://www.autocareerstoday.net

College Professors, Sales and Marketing

OVERVIEW

Sales and marketing professors teach undergraduate and graduate students about sales, marketing, and related subjects at colleges and universities. They lecture classes, lead small seminar groups, and create and grade examinations. They also may conduct research, write for publication, and aid in administration. Approximately 82,000 postsecondary business teachers (including those who specialize in sales and marketing) are employed in the United States.

HISTORY

Sales and marketing classes were not taught at U.S. colleges and universities until the early 1900s. According to *The History of Marketing Thought*, by Robert Bartels, the University of Pennsylvania offered a course titled "The Marketing of Products" in 1905 and the University of Wisconsin offered a course titled "Marketing Methods" in 1910. It was not until 1914 that the first marketing textbook, *Marketing Methods and Salesmanship*, was written by Ralph S. Butler, H. DeBower, and J. G. Jones.

In 1915, the National Association of Teachers of Advertising was founded; it later changed its name to the National Association of Marketing Teachers (NAMT). In 1937, the American Marketing Association was founded as a result of the merger of the NAMT and the American Marketing Society. Today, it is the primary professional organization for marketing professionals and represents "individuals and organizations involved in the practice, teaching, and study of marketing worldwide."

QUICK FACTS

School Subjects
Business
Speech

Personal Skills
Communication/ideas
Helping/teaching

Work Environment
Primarily indoors
Primarily one location

Minimum Education Level
Master's degree

Salary Range
$32,770 to $64,900 to $125,400+

Certification or Licensing
None available

Outlook
Much faster than the average

DOT
090

GOE
12.03.02

NOC
4121

O*NET-SOC
25-1011.00

THE JOB

College and university faculty members teach sales, marketing, and related courses at junior colleges or at four-year colleges and universities. At four-year institutions, most faculty members are assistant professors, associate professors, or full professors. These three types of professorships differ in regards to status, job responsibilities, and salary. Assistant professors are new faculty members who are working to get tenure (status as a permanent professor); they seek to advance to associate and then to full professorships.

Sales and marketing professors perform three main functions: teaching, advising, and research. Their most important responsibility is to teach students. Their role within a college department will determine the level of courses they teach and the number of courses per semester. Most professors work with students at all levels, from college freshmen to graduate students. They may head several classes a semester or only a few a year. Some of their classes will have large enrollment, while graduate seminars may consist of only 12 or fewer students. Though professors may spend fewer than 10 hours a week in the actual classroom, they spend many hours preparing lectures and lesson plans, grading papers and exams, and preparing grade reports. They also schedule office hours during the week to be available to students outside of the lecture hall, and they meet with students individually throughout the semester. Some professors teaching this discipline also work in the field at marketing firms or in the marketing or sales department of a large company.

In the classroom, professors lecture on such topics as marketing research, consumer behavior, sales techniques, marketing management, and marketing communications, as well as teach more advanced classes or concentrations on brand management, integrated marketing communications, international sales and marketing, and sales leadership. They administer exams and assign textbook reading and other research.

Another important responsibility is advising students. Not all faculty members serve as advisers, but those who do must set aside large blocks of time to guide students through the program. Sales and marketing professors who serve as advisers may have any number of students assigned to them, from fewer than 10 to more than 100, depending on the administrative policies of the college. Their responsibility may involve looking over a planned program of studies to make sure students meet requirements for graduation, or it may involve working intensively with each student on many aspects of college life. Some may also help or advise students with job placement after graduation.

The third responsibility of sales and marketing professors is research and publication. Faculty members who are heavily involved in research programs sometimes are assigned a smaller teaching load. Sales and marketing professors publish their research findings or designs in various trade journals. They may also contribute to local newspapers and magazines as marketing experts and write books based on their research or their knowledge and experience in the field. College and university teachers write most textbooks used to teach sales and marketing classes.

Some faculty members eventually rise to the position of department chair, where they govern the affairs of an entire department. Department chairs, faculty, and other professional staff members are aided in their myriad duties by graduate assistants, who may help develop teaching materials, conduct research, give examinations, teach lower-level courses, and carry out other activities.

Some sales and marketing professors may also conduct classes in an extension program. In such a program, they teach evening and weekend courses for the benefit of people who otherwise would not be able to take advantage of the institution's resources. They may travel away from the campus and meet with a group of students at another location. They may work full time for the extension division or may divide their time between on-campus and off-campus teaching.

Distance learning programs, an increasingly popular option for students, give professors the opportunity to use today's technologies to remain in one place while teaching students who are at a variety of locations simultaneously. The professor's duties, like those when teaching correspondence courses conducted by mail, include grading work that students send in at periodic intervals and advising students of their progress. Computers, the Internet, e-mail, and video conferencing, however, are some of the technology tools that allow sales and marketing professors and students to communicate in "real time" in a virtual classroom setting. Meetings may be scheduled during the same time as traditional classes or during evenings and weekends. Professors who do this work are sometimes known as *extension work, correspondence,* or *distance learning instructors.* They may teach online courses in addition to other classes or may have distance learning as their major teaching responsibility.

The *junior college sales and marketing instructor* has many of the same kinds of responsibilities as does the teacher in a four-year college or university. Because junior colleges offer only a two-year program, they teach only undergraduates.

REQUIREMENTS

High School
Your high school's college preparatory program likely includes courses in English, foreign language, mathematics, and government. Courses in business, marketing, and advertising will be extra helpful if you plan to become a sales and marketing professor. In addition, you should take courses in speech to get a sense of what it will be like to lecture to a group of students. Your school's debate team can also help you develop public speaking skills, along with research skills.

Postsecondary Training
At least one advanced degree in sales, marketing, marketing research, or a related field is required to be a professor in a college or university. The master's degree is considered the minimum standard, and graduate work beyond the master's is usually desirable.

In the last year of your undergraduate program, you'll apply to graduate programs in your area of study. Standards for admission to a graduate program can be high and the competition heavy, depending on the school. Once accepted into a program, your responsibilities will be similar to those of your professors—in addition to attending seminars, you'll research, prepare articles for publication, and teach some undergraduate courses.

Other Requirements
You should enjoy reading, writing, and researching. Not only will you spend many years studying in school, but your whole career will be based on communicating your thoughts and ideas. People skills are important because you'll be dealing directly with students, administrators, and other faculty members on a daily basis. You should feel comfortable in a role of authority and possess self-confidence.

EXPLORING

Your high school teachers use many of the same skills as college professors, so talk to them about their careers and their college experiences. You can develop your own teaching experience by volunteering at a community center, working at a day care center, or working at a summer camp. Also, spend some time on a college campus to get a sense of the environment. Write to colleges for their admissions brochures and course catalogs (or check them out online); read about the sales and marketing faculty members and the courses they teach. Before visiting college campuses, make arrangements to speak to professors who teach courses that interest you.

These professors may allow you to sit in on their classes and observe. Also, make appointments with college advisers and with people in the admissions and recruitment offices. If your grades are good enough, you might be able to serve as a teaching assistant during your undergraduate years, which can give you experience leading discussions and grading papers.

EMPLOYERS

Approximately 82,000 postsecondary business teachers (including those who specialize in sales and marketing) are employed in the United States. Employment opportunities vary based on area of study and level of education. With an advanced degree, a number of publications, and a record of good teaching, professors should find opportunities in universities all across the country. There are more than 3,800 colleges and universities in the United States; many of these schools have advertising, sales, and marketing departments or offer related courses. Professors teach in undergraduate and graduate programs. The most sought-after positions are those that offer tenure.

Books to Read

Azar, Brian, and Len Foley. *Your Successful Sales Career.* New York: AMACOM Books, 2006.
Connor, Tim. *Your First Year in Sales: Making the Transition from Total Novice to Successful Professional.* New York: Three Rivers Press, 2001.
Gilmore, Christopher. *Your Sales Career Strategy: An Insider's Guide To Those Considering a Career in Outside Sales.* Charleston, S.C.: BookSurge Publishing, 2008.
Gitomer, Jeffrey H. *The Sales Bible: The Ultimate Sales Resource.* Rev. ed. New York: Collins Business, 2008.
Kim, Gabriel. *Vault Career Guide to Sales & Trading.* 2d ed. New York: Vault Inc., 2008.
Kursmark, Louise M. *Sales and Marketing Resumes for $100,000 Careers.* Indianapolis, Ind.: Jist Publishing, 2004.
Kursmark, Louise M., and Edward R. Newill. *Sales Careers: The Ultimate Guide to Getting a High-Paying Sales Job.* Indianapolis, Ind.: Jist Publishing, 2003.
WetFeet. *Careers in Sales.* San Francisco: WetFeet, 2006.
Wolpert, David K. *Sales and Marketing Careers in the Tech Sector.* Austin, Tex.: Swordfish Communications, LLC, 2008.

STARTING OUT

You should start the process of finding a teaching position while you are in graduate school. The process includes developing a curriculum vitae (a detailed, academic resume), writing for publication, assisting with research, attending conferences, and gaining teaching experience and recommendations. Many students begin applying for teaching positions while finishing their graduate program. For most positions at four-year institutions, you must travel to large conferences where interviews can be arranged with representatives from the universities to which you have applied.

Because of the competition for tenure-track positions, you may have to work for a few years in temporary positions, visiting various schools as an adjunct professor. Some professional associations maintain lists of teaching opportunities in their areas. They may also make lists of applicants available to college administrators looking to fill an available position.

ADVANCEMENT

The normal pattern of advancement is from instructor to assistant professor, to associate professor, to full professor. All four academic ranks are concerned primarily with teaching and research. College faculty members who have an interest in and a talent for administration may be advanced to chair of a department or to dean of their college. A few become college or university presidents or other types of administrators.

The instructor is usually an inexperienced college teacher. He or she may hold a doctorate or may have completed all the Ph.D. requirements except for the dissertation. Most colleges look upon the rank of instructor as the period during which the college is trying out the teacher. Instructors usually are advanced to the position of assistant professors within three to four years. Assistant professors are given up to about six years to prove themselves worthy of tenure, and if they do so, they become associate professors. Some professors choose to remain at the associate level. Others strive to become full professors and receive greater status, salary, and responsibilities.

Most colleges have clearly defined promotion policies from rank to rank for faculty members, and many have written statements about the number of years in which instructors and assistant professors may remain in grade. Administrators in many colleges hope to encourage younger faculty members to increase their skills and competencies and thus to qualify for the more responsible positions of associate professor and full professor.

EARNINGS

Earnings vary by the size of the school, by the type of school (public, private, women's only, for example), and by the level of position the professor holds. According to the U.S. Department of Labor, in 2007, the median salary for postsecondary business teachers (including those who teach marketing) was $64,900, with 10 percent earning $125,400 or more and 10 percent earning $32,770 or less. Business teachers who were employed at four-year colleges and universities had mean annual earnings of $79,100; those employed at junior colleges earned $61,070. Those with the highest earnings tend to be senior tenured faculty; those with the lowest earnings are generally graduate assistants. Professors working on the West Coast and the East Coast and those working at doctorate-granting institutions also tend to have the highest salaries. Many professors try to increase their earnings by completing research, publishing in their field, or teaching additional courses.

Benefits for full-time faculty typically include health insurance and retirement funds and, in some cases, stipends for travel related to research, housing allowances, and tuition waivers for dependents.

WORK ENVIRONMENT

A college or university is usually a pleasant place in which to work. Campuses bustle with all types of activities and events, stimulating ideas, and a young, energetic population. Much prestige comes with success as a professor and scholar; professors have the respect of students, colleagues, and others in their community.

Depending on the size of the department, college professors may have their own office, or they may have to share an office with one or more colleagues. Their department may provide them with a computer, Internet access, and research assistants. Sales and marketing professors are also able to do much of their office work at home. They can arrange their schedule around class hours, academic meetings, and the established office hours when they meet with students. Most college teachers work more than 40 hours each week. Although sales and marketing professors may teach only two or three classes a semester, they spend many hours preparing for lectures, examining student work, and conducting research.

OUTLOOK

The U.S. Department of Labor predicts much faster than average employment growth for college and university professors through

2016. College enrollment is projected to grow due to an increased number of 18- to 24-year-olds, an increased number of adults returning to college, and an increased number of foreign-born students. Retirement of current faculty members will also provide job openings. However, competition for full-time, tenure-track positions at four-year schools will be very strong.

FOR MORE INFORMATION

To read about the issues affecting college professors, contact the following organizations:

American Association of University Professors
1012 14th Street, NW, Suite 500
Washington, DC 20005-3465
Tel: 202-737-5900
Email: aaup@aaup.org
http://www.aaup.org

American Federation of Teachers
555 New Jersey Avenue, NW
Washington, DC 20001-2029
Tel: 202-879-4400
http://www.aft.org

For information on marketing, contact
American Marketing Association
311 South Wacker Drive, Suite 5800
Chicago, IL 60606-6629
Tel: 800-262-1150
http://www.marketingpower.com

Commodities Brokers

QUICK FACTS

School Subjects
Business
Mathematics

Personal Skills
Communication/ideas
Leadership/management

Work Environment
Primarily indoors
Primarily one location

Minimum Education Level
Bachelor's degree

Salary Range
$30,890 to $68,430 to $1,000,000+

Certification or Licensing
Required

Outlook
Much faster than the average

DOT
162

GOE
10.02.02

NOC
1113

O*NET-SOC
41-3031.00, 41-3031.01

OVERVIEW

Commodities brokers, also known as *futures commission merchants,* act as agents in carrying out purchases and sales of commodities for customers or traders. Commodities are primary goods that are either raw or partially refined. Such goods are produced by farmers, such as corn, wheat, or cattle, or mined from the earth, such as gold, copper, or silver. Brokers, who may work at a brokerage house, on the floor of a commodities exchange, or independently, are paid a fee or commission for acting as the middleman to conduct and complete the trade. Approximately 320,000 securities, commodities, and financial services sales agents (a group including commodities brokers) are employed in the United States.

HISTORY

In medieval Europe, business was transacted at local market fairs, and commodities, primarily agricultural, were traded at scheduled times and places. As market fairs grew, "fair letters" were set up as a currency representing a future cash settlement for a transaction. With these letters, merchants could travel from one fair to another. This was the precursor to the Japanese system, in which landowners used "certificates of receipt" for their rice crops. As the certificates made their way into the economy, the Dojima Rice Market was established and became the first place where traders bought and sold contracts for the future delivery of rice.

"Forward contracts" entered the U.S. marketplace in the early 19th century. Farmers, swept up in the boom of industrial growth, transportation, and commerce, began to arrange for the future sale of their crops. Traders entered the market along with the development of these contracts. However, there were no regulations to oversee that the commodity was actually delivered or that it was of an acceptable quality. Furthermore, each transaction was an individual business deal because the terms of each contract were variable. To address these issues, the Chicago Board of Trade was formed in 1848, and by 1865 it had set up standards and rules for trading "to arrive" contracts, now known as commodity futures contracts. In 2007, the Chicago Board of Trade merged with the Chicago Mercantile Exchange to become the CME Group.

THE JOB

A futures contract is an agreement to deliver a particular commodity, such as wheat, pork bellies, or coffee, at a specific date, time, and place. For example, a farmer might sell his oats before they are sowed (known as hedging) because he cannot predict what kind of price he will be able to demand later on. If the weather is favorable and crops are good, he will have competition, which will drive prices down. If there is a flood or drought, oats will be scarce, driving the price up. He wants to ensure a fair price for his product to protect his business and limit his risk, since he cannot predict what will happen.

On the other side of the equation is the user of the oats, perhaps a cereal manufacturer, who purchases these contracts for a delivery of oats at some future date. Producers and users do not correspond to a one-to-one ratio, and the broker is a middleman who does the buying and selling of contracts between the two groups. Brokers may place orders to buy or sell contracts for themselves, for individual clients, or for companies, all of which hope to make a profit by correctly anticipating the direction of a commodity's price. Brokers are licensed to represent clients, and brokers' first responsibility is to take care of their clients' orders before doing trading for themselves. *Traders* also buy and sell contracts for themselves. Unlike brokers, however, they are not licensed (and thus not allowed) to do this work for clients.

When placing a trade for others, brokers are paid a fee or a commission for acting as the agent in making the sale. There are two broad categories of brokers, though they are becoming less distinct. *Full service brokers* provide considerable research to clients, offer price quotes, give trading advice, and assist the customer in making trading decisions. *Discount brokers* simply fill the orders as directed by clients. Some brokers offer intermediate levels of optional services on a sliding scale of commission, such as market research and strategic advice.

In general, brokers are responsible for taking and carrying out all commodity orders and being available on call to do so; reporting back to the client upon fulfilling the order request; keeping the client abreast of breaking news; maintaining account balances and other financial data; and obtaining market information when needed and informing the client about important changes in the marketplace.

A commodities broker in the crude oil pit at the New York Mercantile Exchange makes a trade. *(Monika Graff, The Image Works)*

Brokers can work on the floor of a commodity futures exchange—the place where contracts are bought and sold—for a brokerage house, or independently. The exchange has a trading floor where brokers transact their business in the trading pit. There are 11 domestic exchanges, with the main ones in Chicago, Kansas City, New York, and Minneapolis. To be allowed to work on the floor, a broker must have a membership (also known as a "seat") in the exchange or must be employed by a company with a seat in the exchange, which is a private organization. Memberships are limited to a specific number, and seats may be rented or purchased. Although seat prices vary due to factors such as the health of the overall economy and the type of seat being purchased, they are all extremely expensive. Seat prices can range from tens of thousands of dollars to hundreds of thousands of dollars (full seats have been known to sell for $700,000 and more). Naturally, this expense alone limits the number of individuals who can become members. In addition to being able to afford a seat, candidates for membership to any exchange must undergo thorough investigations of their credit standings, financial backgrounds, characters, and understanding of trading.

Most brokers do not have seats but work for brokerage houses that deal in futures. Examples of these houses include Merrill Lynch or Morgan Stanley, which deal in stocks, bonds, commodities, and other investments, and smaller houses, such as R.J. O'Brien and Associates LLC, that handle only commodities.

Companies can also have a seat on the exchange, and they have their own *floor brokers* in the pit to carry out trades for the brokerage house. Brokers in the company take orders from the public for buying or selling a contract and promptly pass it on to the floor broker in the pit of the exchange. Brokers also have the choice of running their own business. Known as *introducing brokers,* they handle their own clients and trades and use brokerage houses to place their orders. Introducing brokers earn a fee by soliciting business trades, but they don't directly handle the customer's funds.

REQUIREMENTS
High School
A bachelor's degree is required for most brokers' positions. Commodities brokers need to have a wide range of knowledge, covering such areas as economics, world politics, and sometimes even the weather. To begin to develop this broad base of knowledge, start in high school by taking history, math, science, and business classes. Since commodities brokers are constantly working with people to

make a sale, take English classes to enhance your communication skills. In addition to this course work, you might also consider getting a part-time job working in a sales position. Such a job will also give you the chance to hone your communication and sales skills.

Postsecondary Training
The majority of brokers have a college degree, especially those working for large firms. While there is no "commodities broker major," you can improve your chances of obtaining a job in this field by studying economics, finance, or business administration while in college. Keep in mind that you should continue to develop your understanding of politics and technologies, so government and computer classes will also be useful.

Brokerage firms look for employees who have sales ability, strong communication skills, and self-confidence. Commodities is often a second career for many people who have demonstrated these qualities in other positions.

Certification or Licensing
To become a commodities broker, it is necessary to pass the National Commodities Futures Examination (the Series 3 exam) to become eligible to satisfy the registration requirements of federal, state, and industry regulatory agencies. The test covers market and trading knowledge as well as rules and regulations and is composed of true/false and multiple-choice questions. Registration for the exam is through the Financial Industry Regulatory Authority. Preparation materials are available through a number of sources, such as the Institute for Financial Markets (http://www.theifm.org). Brokers must also register with the National Futures Association.

Other Requirements
To be a successful broker, you must possess a combination of research and money management skills. You need to be attentive to detail and have a knack for analyzing data. Strong communications and sales skills are important as well, as brokers make money by convincing people to let them place their trades. An interest in and awareness of the world around you will also be a contributing factor to your success in this field, as commodities are influenced by everything from political decisions and international news to social and fashion trends.

You must also be emotionally stable to work in such a volatile environment. You need to be persistent, aggressive, and comfortable taking risks and dealing with failure. Strong, consistent, and independent judgment is also key. You must be a disciplined hard worker, able to comb through reams of market reports and charts to gain a thorough understanding of a particular commodity and the mechanics of the marketplace. You also need to be outspoken and assertive and able to yell out prices loudly and energetically on the trading floor and to command attention.

EXPLORING

Students interested in commodities trading should visit one of the futures exchanges. All of them offer public tours, and you'll get to see up close just how the markets work and the roles of the players involved. All the exchanges offer educational programs and publications, and most have a Web site. The CME Group publishes *An Introduction to Futures and Options,* the full text of which, along with many other educational handbooks and pamphlets, is available at http://www.cmegroup.com/education/interactive/introduction. There are hundreds of industry newsletters and magazines available (such as *Futures Magazine,* available at http://www.futuresmag.com), and many offer free samples of publications or products. Read what trading advisers have to say and how they say it. Learn their lingo and gain an understanding of the marketplace. If you have any contacts in the industry, arrange to spend a day with a broker. Watch him or her at work, and you'll learn how orders are entered, processed, and reported.

Do your own research. Adopt a commodity, chart its prices, test some of your own ideas, and analyze the marketplace. There are also a variety of inexpensive software programs, as well as Web sites, that simulate trading.

Finally, consider a job as a *runner* during the summer before your freshman year in college. Runners transport the order, or "paper," from the phone clerk to the broker in the pit and relay information to and from members on the floor. This is the single best way to get hands-on experience in the industry.

EMPLOYERS

Approximately 320,000 securities, commodities, and financial services sales agents (a group including commodities brokers) are employed in the United States. Commodities brokers work on the floor of a commodity futures exchange, for brokerage houses, or independently.

STARTING OUT

College graduates can start working with a brokerage house as an associate and begin handling stocks. After several years they can take the certification exam and move into futures. Another option is to start as support staff, either at the exchange or the brokerage house. Sales personnel try to get customers to open accounts, and account executives develop and service customers for the brokerage firm. At the exchange, *phone clerks* receive incoming orders and communicate the information to the runners. Working in the back as an accountant, money manager, or member of the research staff is also another route. School career services offices may be able to assist graduates in finding jobs with brokerage houses. Applications may also be made directly to brokerage houses.

Many successful brokers and traders began their careers as runners, and each exchange has its own training program. Though the pay is low, runners learn the business very quickly with a hands-on experience not available in an academic classroom. Contact one of the commodities exchanges for information on becoming a runner.

ADVANCEMENT

A broker who simply executes trades can advance to become a full-service broker. Through research and analysis and the accumulation of experience and knowledge about the industry, a broker can advance from an order filler and become a commodity trading adviser. A broker can also become a money manager and make all trading decisions for clients.

Within the exchange, a broker can become a *floor manager,* overseeing the processes of order taking and information exchange. To make more money, a broker can also begin to place his or her own trades for his or her own private account, though the broker's first responsibility is to the customers.

EARNINGS

This is an entrepreneurial business. A broker's commission is based on the number of clients he or she recruits, the amount of money they invest, and the profit they make. The sky's the limit. In recent years, the most successful broker made $25 million. A typical salary for a newly hired employee in a brokerage might average $1,500 per month plus a 30 percent commission on sales. Smaller firms are likely to pay a smaller commission. The U.S. Department of Labor reports that the median annual earnings for securities, commodities, and financial services sales representatives (a group including commodities brokers) were $68,430 in 2007. The lowest paid 10 percent earned less than $30,890; the highest paid 10 percent earned more than $145,600 annually.

Benefits vary but are usually very good at large employers. For example, those working at one of the world's leading futures exchanges enjoy benefits such as vacation and sick days; medical, life, and disability insurance; and flextime during summer months. Full tuition reimbursement may also be available, as well as a company-matched savings plan, a tax-deferred savings plan, and a pension program.

WORK ENVIRONMENT

A growing number of exchanges now use electronic systems to automate trades, and many use them exclusively. At exchanges that still use the "open outcry" system, the trading floor is noisy and chaotic. Every broker must be an auctioneer, yelling out his own price bids for purchases and sales. The highest bid wins and silences all the others. When a broker's primal scream is not heard, bids and offers can also be communicated with hand signals.

Brokers stand for most of the day, often in the same place, so that traders interested in their commodity can locate them easily. Each broker wears a distinctly colored jacket with a prominent identification badge. The letter on the badge identifies the broker and appears on the paperwork relating to the trade. Members of the exchange and employees of member firms wear red jackets. Some brokers and traders also have uniquely patterned jackets to further increase their visibility in the pit.

Brokers and traders do not have a nine-to-five job. While commodities trading on the exchange generally takes place from 9:00 A.M. to 1:00 P.M., international trading runs from 2:45 P.M. to 6:50 A.M.

In the rough and tumble world of the futures exchange, emotions run high as people often win or lose six- or seven-figure amounts within hours. Tension is fierce, the pace is frantic, and angry, verbal, and sometimes physical exchanges are not uncommon.

OUTLOOK

The U.S. Department of Labor predicts that employment for securities, commodities, and financial services sales agents will grow much faster than the average for all careers through 2016. Growth will result from people expecting high returns on their investments (leading them to increasingly invest in markets), the growing number and increasing complexity of investment options, and the new commodities available for investment due to the increasingly globalized marketplace. Additionally, as people and companies become more interested in and sophisticated about investing, they are entering futures markets and need the services provided by brokers. Baby Boomers are reaching retirement age, and many are looking to invest in markets as a way of saving for their futures; additionally, many women in the workforce and higher household incomes means more investment.

New computer and information technology is rapidly influencing and advancing the industry. Many systems have unique features designed specifically to meet customers' needs. New technology, such as electronic order entry, hookups to overseas exchanges, and night trading, is rapidly evolving, offering brokers new ways to manage risk and provide price information.

Because many people are attracted to this work by the possibility of earning large incomes, competition for jobs is particularly keen. However, job turnover is also fairly high due to the stress of the work and the fact that many beginning brokers are not able to establish a large enough clientele to be profitable. Small brokerage firms may offer the best opportunities for those just starting out in this work.

FOR MORE INFORMATION

This center provides information on workshops, home study courses, educational materials, and publications for futures and securities professionals.
  Center for Futures Education
  PO Box 309
  Grove City, PA 16127-0309
  Tel: 724-458-5860
  Email: info@thectr.com
  http://www.thectr.com

For a general overview of options, visit the Learning Center section of the CBOE Web site.
  Chicago Board Options Exchange (CBOE)
  400 South LaSalle Street
  Chicago, IL 60605-1023
  Tel: 877-843-2263
  http://www.cboe.com

56   Careers in Focus: Sales

CME Group was formed in 2007 as a result of a merger between the Chicago Mercantile Exchange and the Chicago Board of Trade. Visit its Web site for a wide variety of educational programs and materials, and general information on commodities careers.
CME Group
Tel: 800-331-3332
Email: info@cmegroup.com
http://www.cmegroup.com

For information on the commodities futures industry, contact
Commodity Futures Trading Commission
Three Lafayette Centre
1155 21st Street, NW
Washington, DC 20581-0001
Tel: 202-418-5000
Email: questions@cftc.gov
http://www.cftc.gov/cftc/cftchome.htm

For more information on the National Commodities Futures Examination, contact
Financial Industry Regulatory Authority
1735 K Street, NW
Washington, DC 20006-1500
Tel: 301-590-6500
http://www.finra.org

For information on membership, training, and registration, contact
National Futures Association
120 Broadway, #1125
New York, NY 10271-1196
Tel: 212-608-8660
Email: information@nfa.futures.org
http://www.nfa.futures.org

The Learning Center section of the Philadelphia Board of Trade's Web site provides a glossary of terms, suggested reading, and an overview of the financial industry.
Philadelphia Stock Exchange
1900 Market Street
Philadelphia, PA 19103-3584
Tel: 800-843-7459
http://www.phlx.com

Visit the Web sites or contact the following exchanges for general background information about the field:
Intercontinental Exchange
https://www.theice.com

Minneapolis Grain Exchange
http://www.mgex.com

New York Mercantile Exchange
http://www.nymex.com

Computer and Electronics Sales Representatives

QUICK FACTS

School Subjects
Business
Computer science
Speech

Personal Skills
Communication/ideas
Technical/scientific

Work Environment
Primarily indoors
Primarily multiple locations

Minimum Education Level
Bachelor's degree

Salary Range
$14,780 to $20,150 to $91,080+

Certification or Licensing
None available

Outlook
About as fast as the average

DOT
275

GOE
10.02.01, 10.03.01

NOC
6421

O*NET-SOC
41-2031.00, 41-4011.03

OVERVIEW

Computer and electronics sales representatives sell hardware, software, peripheral computer equipment, and electronics equipment to customers and businesses of all sizes. Sometimes they follow up sales with installation of systems, maintenance, or training of the client's staff. They are employed in all aspects of businesses. Sales representatives that work for retail stores deal with consumers. Representatives that specialize in a particular piece of hardware, specific software program, or electronic component may do business with banks, insurance companies, or accounting firms, among others.

HISTORY

The first major advances in modern computer technology were made during World War II. After the war, people thought that computers were too big (they easily filled entire warehouses) to ever be used for anything other than government projects, such as their use in compiling the 1950 census.

The introduction of semiconductors to computer technology made smaller and less expensive computers possible. The semiconductors replaced the bigger, slower vacuum tubes of the first computers. These changes made it easier for businesses to adapt computers to their needs, which they began doing as early as 1954. Within 30 years, computers had revolutionized the way people work, play, and even shop. Few occupations have remained untouched by this technological revolution. Consequently, computers are found in businesses, government offices, hospitals, schools, science labs, and homes. Clearly, there is a huge market for the sale of computers and peripheral equipment. There is an important need today for knowledgeable sales representatives to serve both the retail public and to advise corporations and large organizations on their computer and electronics purchases.

THE JOB

The first step in the selling process, whether the sales environment is retail or corporate, is client consultation. Sales representatives determine the client's current technological needs as well as those of the future. During consultation, reps explain the technology's value and how well it will perform. Often, customers do not have expertise in computer or electronics technology, so the rep must explain and translate complicated computer tech-talk as well as answer numerous questions. In retail computer sales, the customer decides what system, peripheral, or software to purchase and then brings it home or arranges for its delivery.

In the corporate sales environment, client consultations usually take longer, often entailing numerous trips to the client's office or place of business. Ron Corrales, an account support manager for Accenture (formerly Andersen Consulting), acknowledges that client consultation is the crucial first step in the sales process. After the client's business is researched and its needs are assessed, possible solutions are outlined in the form of a written or oral presentation. "I was really nervous the first few times I gave a presentation," recalls Corrales. "After all, these were CEOs and CFOs of Fortune 500 companies!" The talent for public speaking and technical writing frequently comes into play. Sales representatives must be able to effectively and clearly present the product and its capabilities, often in layperson's terms. After perfecting his communications skills, Corrales now thinks of client presentations as "just part of the job."

Accenture is one of the largest information technology (IT) consulting firms in the world. It provides proprietary software used by businesses worldwide. Its programs are tools tailor-made to fit the needs of each company and its specific routines, such as accounting, customer billing, inventory control, and marketing, among others. Its client list includes the grocery store chain Kroger's, Harley Davidson, and the U.S. government.

An electronics sales representative describes the features of a plasma television to two customers. *(The Berkshire Eagle, Caroline Bonnivier, AP Photo)*

After the presentation, if all goes well, Corrales helps draft the contract. Every aspect of the agreement is outlined and specified—the type of software, length of contract, including services, training, or maintenance. The deal is considered "done" once the Accenture partners and company CEOs sign, and of course, the fees are paid. Once the companies receive their software, it is installed, and glitches, if any, are resolved. Many times company employees are trained by Accenture consultants on how to use the software to its fullest capability. Usually a one-year maintenance contract is provided to the client.

To stay abreast of technological advances, sales representatives must attend training sessions or continuing education classes. It also helps to know the essence of each client's field and the nature of its work. Weekly departmental meetings are necessary to learn of any developments or projects within the department or the company as a whole. A big part of Corrales' job is managing his territory, making client calls or visits when necessary. A chunk of his workday is devoted to "putting out potential client 'fires'."

REQUIREMENTS

High School

Classes in speech and writing will help you learn how to communicate your product to large groups of people. Computer science and electronics classes will give you a basic overview of the field. General business and math classes will also be helpful.

Postsecondary Training
Though a small number of computer sales positions may be filled by high school graduates, those jobs are scarce. Most large companies prefer a bachelor's or advanced degree in computer or information science, engineering, business, or marketing.

Prepare yourself for a career in this field by developing your computer knowledge. Take computer and math classes, as well as business classes to help develop a sound business sense. Since sales representatives are often required to meet with clients and make sales presentations, excellent communications skills are a must. Hone yours by taking English and speech classes.

In this particular field of sales, extensive computer knowledge is just as important as business savvy. Most computer sales representatives pursue computer science courses concurrently with their business classes. For computer sales representatives specializing in a specific industry (for example, health care or banking), training in the basics and current issues of that field is needed. Such training can be obtained through special work training seminars, adult education classes, or courses at a technical school. Many companies require their sales staff to complete a training program where they'll learn the technologies and work tools needed for the job. (This is where you'll pick up the techno-speak for your specific field.)

Ron Corrales holds a master's of information science degree. One of the college classes that has helped him the most in his career is "technical writing and communication. It helps to be able to explain complicated and technical material in layperson terms."

Other Requirements
As important as having computer and electronics knowledge is having a "sales" personality. Sales representatives must be confident and knowledgeable about themselves as well as the product they are selling. They should have strong interpersonal skills and enjoy dealing with all types of people, from families buying their first PC, to CEOs of Fortune 500 companies. "People in this business are well rounded and enjoy technology," Corrales adds, "but, to do well, they need to be competitively hungry, and like to talk—a lot!"

EMPLOYERS
Employment opportunities for this field exist nationwide. What are your priorities? Do you want to work for an industry giant? IBM?

Microsoft? Motorola? You may be enticed with attractive perks, such as stock options, a big travel expense account, or graduate school tuition, among other benefits. Note, however, that these are huge corporations; you'll really have to be something special if you want to stand apart from the other applicants. Getting hired is tough, too. Microsoft, for example, receives thousands of resumes weekly.

Middle-size and small companies usually require their employees to don several hats. That means sales representatives may be responsible for entire presentations, including product and client research, as well as maintenance and service. It may sound like too much work, and for some tasks you may feel overqualified. The rewards include being part of the ground team when your company takes off. If it doesn't, you can always chalk it up to good experience.

STARTING OUT

That Ron Corrales had two job offers by graduation is not uncommon, especially for students with computer-related majors. Many top companies recruit aggressively on campus, often enticing soon-to-be grads with signing bonuses or other incentives at school job fairs.

Other avenues to try when conducting your job search include the newspaper job ads and trade papers. Try the Internet, too. Many companies maintain Web sites where they post employment opportunities as well as receive online resumes and applications. Your school's career services office is a great place to start your job search. Not only will the counselors have information on jobs not advertised in the paper, but they can also provide tips on resume writing and interviewing techniques.

ADVANCEMENT

With a good work record, a computer or electronics sales representative may be offered a position in management. A manager is responsible for supervising the sales for a given retail store, sales territory, or corporate branch. A management position comes with not only a higher salary but a higher level of responsibility as well. An effective manager should be well versed in the company's product and selling techniques and be able to keep a sales group working at top capacity. Those already at the management level may decide to transfer to the marketing side of the business. Positions in marketing may involve planning the marketing strategy for a new computer or electronics product or line, and coordinating sales campaigns and product distribution.

EARNINGS

Because computer and electronics sales reps work in a variety of settings, ranging from the local store on Main Street to large corporations, their annual salaries vary greatly. Sales representatives working in retail are paid an hourly wage, usually minimum wage ($7.25 an hour), which may be supplemented with commissions based on a percentage of sales made that day or week. Salaries are also dependent on the product sold (PCs, mainframes, peripherals) and the market served.

According to the U.S. Department of Labor, earnings for all retail sales reps, including commissions, came to a median of $9.69 per hour in 2007. For full-time work, 40 hours a week, this hourly wage translates into a yearly income of approximately $20,150. At the bottom end of the pay scale were those making less than $7.11 per hour (approximately $14,780 annually), and at the top were those who made more than $18.84 hourly (approximately $39,190 annually). Sales representatives, wholesale and manufacturing who specialized in the sale of computer and peripheral equipment had mean annual earnings of $91,080 in 2007.

Computer sales representatives who specialize in corporate sales and installation of hardware or software, like Ron Corrales, tend to earn quite a bit more.

Most computer sales representatives working for large employers are offered a benefits package including health and life insurance, paid holidays and vacations, and continuing education and training, as well as volume bonuses or stock options.

WORK ENVIRONMENT

Retail sales representatives work in a retail environment. A 40-hour workweek is typical, though longer hours may be necessary during busy shopping seasons. Whether or not the sales representative is compensated during these extended hours varies from store to store. However, increased work times usually means increased sales volume, which in the end translates to more commissions. Retail representatives must be prepared to deal with a large volume of customers with varying levels of technical knowledge, all with many questions. It is necessary to treat customers with respect and patience, regardless of the size of the sale, or when there is no sale at all.

Corporate sales representatives, like Ron Corrales, work in a professional office environment. Work is conducted at the home office as well as in the field when making sales calls. Work schedules vary depending on the size of territory and number of clients. A 40-hour workweek is the exception rather than the rule. "I average about

60-plus hours a week," says Corrales. "My hours are flexible, but with a lot of weekend work and travel."

Also, corporate sales representatives should have excellent communications skills, both in person and on the telephone, because they spend a lot of time consulting with clients. Also, good writing skills are needed when producing proposals and sales reports, often under the pressure of a tight deadline.

OUTLOOK

Employment opportunities for all retail sales representatives are expected to grow about as fast as the average for all careers through 2016, according to the U.S. Department of Labor. Employment growth for those in corporate sales is also expected to grow at this rate.

As computer companies continue to price their products competitively, more and more people will be able to afford new home computer systems or upgrade existing ones with the latest hardware, software, and peripherals. Increased retail sales will increase the need for competent and knowledgeable sales representatives. Many jobs exist at retail giants (Best Buy and Office Depot, known for office-related supplies and equipment, are two examples) that provide consumers with good price packages as well as optional services such as installation and maintenance.

Employment opportunities can also be found with computer specialty stores and consulting companies that deal directly with businesses and their corporate computer and application needs. Computers have become an almost indispensable tool for running a successful business, be it an accounting firm, a public relations company, or a multi-physician medical practice. As long as this trend continues, knowledgeable sales representatives will be needed to bring the latest technological advances in hardware and software to the consumer and corporate level.

All sales workers are adversely affected by economic downturns. In a weak economy, consumers purchase fewer expensive items, and businesses look for ways to trim costs. This results in less of a demand for computers and computer accessories and a reduced need for sales workers.

FOR MORE INFORMATION

For information on internships, student membership, and the student magazine, Crossroads, *contact*
    Association for Computing Machinery
    Two Penn Plaza, Suite 701

New York, NY 10121-0701
Tel: 800-342-6626
http://www.acm.org

For industry and membership information, or for a copy of The Representor, *a quarterly trade magazine, contact*
Electronics Representatives Association International
300 West Adams Street, Suite 617
Chicago, IL 60606-5109
Tel: 312-527-3050
Email: info@era.org
http://www.era.org

For industry or membership information, contact
North American Retail Dealers Association
222 South Riverside Plaza, Suite 2160
Chicago, IL 60606-6160
Tel: 800-621-0298
Email: nardasvc@narda.com
http://www.narda.com

Counter and Rental Clerks

QUICK FACTS

School Subjects
English
Mathematics
Speech

Personal Skills
Following instructions
Helping/teaching

Work Environment
Primarily indoors
Primarily one location

Minimum Education Level
High school diploma

Salary Range
$14,400 to $20,070 to $38,620+

Certification or Licensing
Voluntary

Outlook
Much faster than the average

DOT
279

GOE
09.05.01

NOC
1453

O*NET-SOC
41-2021.00

OVERVIEW

Counter and rental clerks work as intermediaries between the general public and businesses that provide goods and services. They take orders and receive payments for such services as DVD rentals, automobile rentals, and laundry and dry cleaning. They often assist customers with their purchasing or rental decisions, especially when sales personnel are not available. These workers might also prepare billing statements, keep records of receipts and sales, and balance money in their cash registers. There are more than 477,000 counter and rental clerks working in the United States.

HISTORY

The first retail outlets in the United States sold food staples, farm necessities, and clothing, and many also served as the post office and became the social and economic centers of their communities. Owners of these general stores often performed all the jobs in the business.

Over the years retailing has undergone numerous changes. Large retail stores, requiring many workers, including counter and rental clerks, became more common. Also emerging were specialized retail or chain outlets—clothing stores, bicycle shops, computer shops, video stores, and athletic footwear boutiques—which also needed counter and rental clerks to assist customers and to receive payment for services or products.

THE JOB

Job duties vary depending on the type of business. In a shoe repair shop, for example, the clerk receives the shoes to be repaired or cleaned from the customer, examines the shoes, gives a price quote and a receipt to the customer, and then sends the shoes to the work department for the necessary repairs or cleaning. The shoes are marked with a tag specifying what work needs to be done and to whom the shoes belong. After the work is completed, the clerk returns the shoes to the customer and collects payment.

In stores where customers rent equipment or merchandise, clerks prepare rental forms and quote rates to customers. The clerks answer customer questions about the operation of the equipment. They often take a deposit to cover any accidents or possible damage. Clerks also check the equipment to be certain it is in good working order and make minor adjustments, if necessary. With long-term rentals, such as storage-facility rentals, clerks notify the customers when the rental period is about to expire and when the rent is overdue. Video-rental clerks greet customers, check out DVDs, and accept payment. Upon return of the DVDs, the clerks check the condition of the DVDs and then put them back on the shelves.

In smaller shops with no sales personnel or in situations when the sales personnel are unavailable, counter and rental clerks assist customers with purchases or rentals by demonstrating the merchandise, answering customers' questions, accepting payment, recording sales, and wrapping the purchases or arranging for their delivery.

In addition to these duties, clerks sometimes prepare billing statements to be sent to customers. They might keep records of receipts and sales throughout the day and balance the money in their registers when their work shift ends. They sometimes are responsible for the display and presentation of products in their store. In supermarkets and grocery stores, clerks stock shelves and bag food purchases for the customers.

Service-establishment attendants work in various types of businesses, such as a laundry, where attendants take clothes to be cleaned or repaired and write down the customer's name and address. *Watch-and-clock-repair clerks* receive clocks and watches for repair and examine the timepieces to estimate repair costs. They might make minor repairs, such as replacing a watchband; otherwise, the timepiece is forwarded to the repair shop with a description of needed repairs.

Many clerks have job titles that describe what they do and where they work. These include laundry-pricing clerks, photo-finishing-counter clerks, tool-and-equipment-rental clerks, airplane-charter

A rental-car agent helps a customer complete paperwork to rent a car. *(Geri Engberg, The Image Works)*

clerks, baby-stroller and wheelchair-rental clerks, storage-facility-rental clerks, boat-rental clerks, trailer-rental clerks, automobile-rental clerks, fur-storage clerks, and self-service-laundry and dry-cleaning attendants.

REQUIREMENTS

High School
High school courses useful for the job include English, speech, and mathematics, as well as any business-related classes, such as typing, computer science, and those covering principles in retailing. Although there are no specific educational requirements for clerk positions, most employers prefer to hire high school graduates. Legible handwriting and the ability to add and subtract numbers quickly are also necessary.

Certification or Licensing
The National Retail Federation offers the following voluntary certifications for counter and rental clerks: national professional certification in customer service, national professional certification in sales, and basics of retail credential. Contact the federation for more information.

Other Requirements

To be a counter and rental clerk, you should have a pleasant personality and an ability to interact with a variety of people. You should also be neat and well groomed and have a high degree of personal responsibility. Counter and rental clerks must be able to adjust to alternating periods of heavy and light activity. No two days—or even customers—are alike. Because some customers can be rude or even hostile, you must exercise tact and patience at all times.

EXPLORING

There are numerous opportunities for part-time or temporary work as a clerk, especially during the holiday season. Many high schools have developed work-study programs that combine courses in retailing with part-time work in the field. Store owners cooperating in these programs may hire you as a full-time worker after you complete the course.

EMPLOYERS

Of the numerous types of clerks working in the United States, approximately 477,000 work as counter and rental clerks at video rental stores, dry cleaners, car rental agencies, and other such establishments. These are not the only employers of clerks, however; hardware stores, shoe stores, moving businesses, camera stores—in fact, nearly any business that sells goods or provides services to the general public employs clerks. Many work on a part-time basis.

STARTING OUT

If you are interested in securing an entry-level position as a clerk, you should contact stores directly. Workers with some experience, such as those who have completed a work-study program in high school, should have the greatest success, but most entry-level positions do not require any previous experience. Jobs are often listed in help-wanted advertisements.

Most stores provide new workers with on-the-job training in which experienced clerks explain company policies and procedures and teach new employees how to operate the cash register and other necessary equipment. This training usually continues for several weeks until the new employee feels comfortable on the job.

ADVANCEMENT

Counter and rental clerks usually begin their employment doing routine tasks, such as checking stock and operating the cash register. With experience, they might advance to more complicated assignments and assume some sales responsibilities. Those with the skill and aptitude might become salespeople or store managers, although further education is normally required for management positions.

The high turnover rate in clerk positions increases the opportunities for being promoted. The number and kind of opportunities, however, depend on the place of employment and the ability, training, and experience of the employee.

EARNINGS

According to the U.S. Department of Labor, the median hourly wage for counter and rental clerks was $9.65 in 2007. Working year round at 40 hours per week, a clerk earning this wage would make approximately $20,070 annually. Of all counter and rental clerks, 10 percent earned less than $6.92 per hour (approximately $14,400 annually) in 2007, and 10 percent earned more than $18.57 per hour (or $38,620 annually). Wages among clerks vary for a number of reasons, including the industry in which they work. The Department of Labor reports, for example, that those working in the automobile equipment rental and leasing field had mean hourly earnings of $11.90 (approximately $24,740 per year) in 2007, while those in dry cleaning and laundry services earned a mean of $8.79 per hour (approximately $18,280 yearly). Wages also vary among clerks due to factors such as size of the business, location in the country, and experience of the employee.

Those workers who have union affiliation (usually those who work for supermarkets) may earn considerably more than their nonunion counterparts. Full-time workers, especially those who are union members, might also receive benefits such as paid vacation time and health insurance, but this is not the industry norm. Some businesses offer merchandise discounts for their employees. Part-time workers usually receive fewer benefits than those working full time.

WORK ENVIRONMENT

Although a 40-hour workweek is common, many stores operate on a 44- to 48-hour workweek. Most stores are open on Saturday and many on Sunday. Most stores are also open one or more weekday evenings, so a clerk's working hours might vary from week to week and include evening and weekend shifts. Many counter and rental clerks work overtime during Christmas and other rush seasons. Part-time clerks generally work during peak business periods.

Most clerks work indoors in well-ventilated and well-lighted environments. The job can be routine and repetitive, and clerks often spend much of their time on their feet.

OUTLOOK

The U.S. Department of Labor predicts that employment for counter and rental clerks will grow much faster than the average for all occupations through 2016. Businesses that focus on customer service will always want to hire friendly and responsible clerks. Major employers should be those providing rental products and services, such as car rental firms, video rental stores, and other equipment rental businesses. Because of the high turnover in this field, however, many job openings will come from the need to replace workers. Opportunities for temporary or part-time work should be good, especially during busy business periods. Employment opportunities for clerks are plentiful in large metropolitan areas, where their services are in great demand.

FOR MORE INFORMATION

For information on scholarships and internships, or industry certification, contact
Retail Industry Leaders Association
1700 North Moore Street, Suite 2250
Arlington, VA 22209-1933
Tel: 703-841-2300
http://www.retail-leaders.org/new/index.aspx

For information about careers in the retail industry and certification, contact
National Retail Federation
325 Seventh Street, NW, Suite 1100
Washington, DC 20004-2818
Tel: 800-673-4692
http://www.nrf.com

Financial Services Brokers

QUICK FACTS

School Subjects
Business
Mathematics

Personal Skills
Communication/ideas
Technical/scientific

Work Environment
Primarily indoors
Primarily one location

Minimum Education Level
Bachelor's degree

Salary Range
$30,890 to $68,430 to $122,260+

Certification or Licensing
Required by certain states

Outlook
Much faster than the average

DOT
250

GOE
13.01.01

NOC
1113

O*NET-SOC
41-3031.00, 41-3031.01

OVERVIEW

Financial services brokers, sometimes called *registered representatives, account executives, financial consultants, financial specialists, securities sales representatives,* or *stockbrokers,* work to represent both individuals and organizations who wish to invest in and sell stocks, bonds, or other financial products. Financial services brokers analyze companies offering stocks to see if investing is worth the risk. They also advise clients on proper investment strategies for their own investment goals. Securities, commodities, and financial services brokers hold approximately 320,000 jobs in the United States.

HISTORY

When a government wants to build a new sewer system or a company wants to build a new factory, it rarely has the required money—or capital—readily at hand to do it. It must first raise the capital from investors. Historically, raising capital to finance the needs of government and commerce was—and often still is—an arduous task. European monarchies, particularly during the 18th and 19th centuries, relied heavily upon bankers to meet the costs of the interminable wars that devastated the continent and to assist in early industrial expansion. This system grew obsolete, however, and governments, banks, and industry turned to the burgeoning middle class for funds. They offered middle class investors securities and stocks—a fractional ownership in a company or enterprise—in exchange for their money. Soon, dealers emerged that linked government and industry with the smaller investor. In the United States, the New York Stock Exchange was formed in 1790 and officially established in 1817.

The stock exchange functions as a marketplace where stockbrokers buy and sell securities for individuals or institutions. Stock prices can fluctuate from minute to minute, with the price of a stock at any given time determined by the demand for it. As a direct result of the disastrous stock market crash of 1929, the Federal Securities Act of 1934 set up a federal commission to control the handling of securities and made illegal any manipulation of prices on stock exchanges. Today, the public is protected by regulations that set standards for stock listings, require public disclosure of the financial condition of companies offering stock, and prohibit stock manipulation and trading on inside information.

THE JOB

The most important part of a broker's job is finding customers and building a client base. Beginning brokers spend much of their time searching for customers, relying heavily on telephone solicitation such as "cold calls"—calling people with whom they have never had any contact. Brokers also find customers through business and social contacts or they might be given a list of likely prospects from their brokerage firm.

When financial services brokers open accounts for new customers, they first record all the personal information that is required to allow the customer to trade securities through the brokerage firm. Depending on a customer's knowledge of the market, the broker may explain the meaning of stock market terms and trading practices and offer financial counseling. Then the broker helps the customer to devise an individual financial portfolio, including securities, life insurance, corporate and municipal bonds, mutual funds, certificates of deposit, annuities, and other investments. The broker must determine the customer's investment goals—such as whether the customer wants long-term, steady growth or a quick turnaround of stocks for short-term gains—and then offers advice on investments accordingly. Once an investment strategy has been developed, brokers execute buy and sell orders for their customers by relaying the information to the floor of the stock exchange, where the order is put into effect by the broker's floor representative. Securities traders also buy and sell securities, but usually as a representative of a private firm.

From the research department of the brokerage firm, brokers obtain information on the activities and projected growth of any company that is currently offering stock or plans to offer stock in the near future. The actual or perceived strength of a company is a major factor in a stock-purchase decision. Brokers must be prepared to answer questions on the technical aspects of stock market operations and also be informed on current economic conditions. They are expected to have the market knowledge to anticipate certain trends and to counsel customers accordingly in terms of their particular stock holdings.

Some financial services brokers specialize in areas such as institutional accounts, bond issues, or mutual funds. Whatever their area of specialization, financial services brokers must keep abreast of all significant political and economic conditions that might effect financial markets, maintain very accurate records for all transactions, and continually solicit new customers.

REQUIREMENTS
High School
If you are interested in becoming a financial services broker, you should take courses in business, accounting, economics, mathematics, government, and communications.

Postsecondary Training
Because of the specialized knowledge necessary to perform this job properly, a college education is increasingly important, especially in the larger brokerage houses. To make intelligent and insightful judgments, a broker must be able to read and understand financial reports and evaluate statistics. For this reason, although employers seldom require specialized academic training, a bachelor's degree in business administration, economics, accounting, or finance is helpful.

Certification or Licensing
Almost all states require brokers to be licensed. Some states administer written examinations and some require brokers to post a personal bond. Brokers must register as representatives of their firms with the Financial Industry Regulatory Authority (FINRA). In order to register with FINRA, brokers must first pass the General Securities Registered Representative Examination (Series 7 exam) to demonstrate competence in the areas in which they will work. In addition, they must be employees of a registered firm for at least four months.

Many states also require brokers to take and pass a second examination—the Uniform Securities Agents State Law Examination.

Other Requirements
Because they deal with the public, brokers should be well groomed and pleasant and have large reserves of tact and patience. Employers look for ambitious individuals with sales ability. Brokers also need self-confidence and the ability to handle frequent rejections. Above all, they must have a highly developed sense of responsibility, because in many instances they will be handling funds that represent a client's life savings.

EXPLORING

Any sales experience can provide you with a general background for work in financial services. You might be able to find summer employment in a brokerage house. A visit to a local investment office, the New York Stock Exchange, or one of the commodities exchanges located in other major cities will provide a valuable opportunity to observe how transactions are handled and what is required of people in the field.

EMPLOYERS

Financial services brokers and related workers hold approximately 320,000 jobs. The U.S. Department of Labor reports that more than 50 percent work for securities and commodities firms, exchanges, and investment services companies. Banks, savings institutions, and credit unions employ one in five. Approximately 17 percent of financial services brokers are self-employed.

Financial services brokers work all around the country. Although many employers are very small, the largest employers of financial services brokers are a few large firms that have their main offices in major cities, especially New York.

STARTING OUT

Many firms hire beginning sales workers and train and retain them for a probationary period to determine their talents and ability to succeed in the business. The training period lasts about six months and includes classroom instruction and on-the-job training. Applications for these beginning jobs may be made directly to the personnel offices of the various securities firms. Check your local Yellow Pages or the Internet for listings of securities firms.

ADVANCEMENT

Depending upon their skills and ambitions, financial services brokers may advance rapidly in this field. Accomplished brokers may find that the size and number of accounts they service will increase to a point at which they no longer need to solicit new customers. Others become branch managers, research analysts, or partners in their own firms.

EARNINGS

The salaries of trainees and beginners range from $1,200 to $1,500 per month, although larger firms pay a somewhat higher starting wage. Once the financial services broker has acquired a sufficient number of accounts, he or she works solely on a commission basis, with fees resulting from the size and type of security bought or sold. Some firms pay annual bonuses to their brokers when business warrants. Since earnings can fluctuate greatly based on the condition of the market, some brokers may find it necessary to supplement their income through other means during times of slow market activity.

According to the U.S. Department of Labor, the median earnings for brokers were $68,430 a year in 2007. The lowest paid 10 percent earned less than $30,890, and the highest paid 10 percent earned more than $145,600.

Benefits for full-time workers include vacation and sick time, health, and sometimes dental, insurance, and pension or 401(k) accounts. Self-employed financial services brokers must provide their own benefits.

WORK ENVIRONMENT

Brokers work more flexible hours than workers in other fields. They may work fewer hours during slow trading periods but be required to put in overtime dealing with paperwork during busy periods.

The atmosphere of a brokerage firm is frequently highly charged, and the peaks and drops of market activity can produce a great deal of tension. Watching fortunes being made is exciting, but the reverse occurs frequently, too, and it requires responsibility and maturity to weather the setbacks.

OUTLOOK

The U.S. Department of Labor predicts that job opportunities for financial services brokers are expected to grow much faster than the average for all occupations through 2016 because of continued interest in the stock market and the increasing number and variety of financial products. Rising personal incomes and greater inherited wealth are increasing the amount of funds people are able to invest. Many people dabble in investing via their personal computers and the Internet. Even those with limited means have the option of investing through a variety of methods such as investment clubs, mutual funds, and monthly payment plans. In addition, the expansion of business activities and new technological breakthroughs will create increased demand for the sale of stock to meet capital requirements for companies around the world.

Demand for financial services brokers fluctuates with the economy. Turnover among beginners is high because they have a hard time soliciting enough clients. Because of potentially high earnings, competition in this business is very intense.

FOR MORE INFORMATION

For information on industry regulation, contact
Financial Industry Regulatory Authority
1735 K Street, NW
Washington, DC 20006-1500
Tel: 301-590-6500
http://www.finra.org

To learn more about investing, the securities industry, and industry issues, contact
Securities Industry and Financial Markets Association
120 Broadway, 35th Floor
New York, NY 10271-0080
Tel: 212-313-1200
http://www.sifma.org

Insurance Agents and Brokers

QUICK FACTS

School Subjects
Business
Mathematics

Personal Skills
Communication/ideas
Leadership/management

Work Environment
Primarily indoors
One location with some travel

Minimum Education Level
Some postsecondary training

Salary Range
$25,230 to $44,110 to $113,190+

Certification or Licensing
Voluntary (certification)
Required by all states (licensing)

Outlook
About as fast as the average

DOT
250

GOE
08.01.02

NOC
6231

O*NET-SOC
41-3021.00

OVERVIEW

Insurance agents and brokers sell policies that provide life, health, and property and casualty insurance; retirement income; and various other types of insurance to new clients or to established policyholders. Some agents are referred to as *underwriters,* since they may be required to estimate insurance risks on some policies. Some agents also sell mutual funds, annuities, and securities and offer estate and retirement planning. Approximately 436,000 insurance agents and brokers work in the United States.

HISTORY

The insurance industry provides protection for its customers against financial loss from various hazards. This protection is offered in the form of insurance policies. The industry is a massive, highly complex one that has grown out of an ancient and very simple principle: the more people who share a financial risk, the smaller the risk is for each.

A crude but effective form of insurance based on this principle was applied thousands of years ago in China. Boats often sank in the treacherous Yangtze River, and cargoes were lost, sometimes bringing financial ruin to their owners. Then the shippers hit on the idea of sharing the risk by having each person's goods distributed among many boats. That way, if one boat sank, a number of people lost a small part of their belongings, but no one person suffered a heavy loss.

The early Babylonians had a form of credit insurance. The Code of Hammurabi, a collection of Babylonian laws written around 1800 B.C. stipulated that a borrower did not have to repay a loan if personal misfortune made it a hardship to do so. The borrower paid an additional amount for this protection.

Another form of insurance made life a little less hazardous for American settlers in the early frontier days. If a family's cabin burned, the neighbors would get together and build them a new one, knowing that they would get the same kind of help if the tables were turned. In a way, they too were sharing the risk.

Today, the population is much too large and life is much too complicated for such simple means of sharing the risk to protect people against the many hazards that could cost them their property or their financial security. Instead, people share the risks by purchasing insurance policies. Customers pay a certain amount of money, called a premium, to an insurance company for coverage against possible loss.

When a person buys a fire insurance policy on a home, for example, he or she pays the insurance company only a small fraction of what it would cost to replace the house. If the house burns down, however, the insurance company is able to pay the owner for all or part of the loss by using the money that many other people have paid for their insurance policies. In that way, each person who buys an insurance policy is protected against financial loss by all of the others who have bought policies.

Employment opportunities in the insurance industry can be found anywhere in the country. In small communities, however, employment is usually limited to agents, brokers, and the clerical workers they employ. The others, such as actuaries, underwriters, and insurance attorneys, work mostly in larger cities, in home offices or regional offices of the insurance companies or industry organizations. These offices are in cities throughout the country, but the greatest number are concentrated in New York, New Jersey, Massachusetts, Connecticut, and Illinois.

THE JOB

The insurance industry is divided into three main branches: life insurance, health insurance, and property and casualty insurance. Companies may specialize in one or all three types of coverage.

Life Insurance. Life insurance is basically a means by which one person provides for the financial security of others, usually other family members, in the event of that person's death. Using life insurance in its simplest form, a person pays an insurance company a small amount on a regular basis (monthly, semianually, annually) for a policy that guarantees that the family will receive a relatively large amount of money if the person dies while covered by the policy. However, many life insurance policies combine this form of protection with others. Some provide for the policyholder to receive a regular income after reaching retirement age. Some provide funds for a college education for the policyholder's children. Some will pay off the mortgage on a person's home if he or she dies or becomes unable to work.

A new type of insurance being offered by some life insurance companies is critical care insurance. This insurance helps defray the costs of treatment for cancer and other critical illnesses. With medical advances and more patients surviving years with critical illnesses, this insurance provides benefits for patients and their families while the insured is still alive instead of only providing for the family upon the death of the insured.

Health Insurance. Health insurance pays all or part of hospitalization, surgery, medicine, and other medical costs. This helps protect the policyholder against large medical bills in the case of an illness or accident.

In Canada and other countries, people are covered by government health insurance. In the United States, health insurance is usually provided by insurance companies or managed care plans, which include health maintenance organizations (HMOs) and preferred provider organizations (PPOs). Usually, an employer pays part of the insurance premiums for employees. The government helps defray medical costs for the elderly and disabled through the Medicare program and for the poor through Medicaid. Supplemental medical insurance is often purchased to cover some costs not covered by Medicare.

Property and Casualty Insurance. Property and casualty insurance comes in a wide variety of forms. It includes the different kinds of insurance that protect people from financial loss if their property is destroyed, damaged, or stolen. It also includes all forms of liability insurance, the insurance that protects people from financial loss if they are responsible for injury to another person or damage to another person's property. An example of liability insurance is medical malpractice insurance.

Within the property and casualty field, there are several specialized branches, or lines, of insurance. Some companies write all lines, while others write only one. In addition to insurance on homes, business places, automobiles, and personal property, this field includes marine insurance, which covers boats and ships and their cargoes, and inland marine insurance, which covers almost anything capable of being transported or which is used in transportation. Inland marine insurance covers everything from furs and paintings to locomotives and bridges.

Also included in the property and casualty field is worker's compensation insurance, which pays a person for loss of wages and medical expenses if he or she is disabled because of an injury or illness connected with a job. Worker's compensation also provides death benefits for dependents if death is due to a work-connected injury or illness. Fidelity bonds, which protect an employer from loss due to dishonesty of an employee, and surety bonds, which guarantee that contracts will be carried out properly, are other forms of insurance written by property and liability companies.

Insurance agents act as field sales representatives for the companies to which they are under contract. They may be under direct contract or work through a general agent who holds a contract. Insurance brokers represent the insurance buyer and do not sell for a particular company but place insurance policies for their clients with the company that offers the best rate and coverage. In addition, some brokers obtain several types of insurance (automobile, household, medical, and so on) to provide a more complete service package for their clients.

The agent's work may be divided into five functions: identifying and soliciting prospects, explaining services, developing insurance plans, closing the transaction, and following up.

The insurance agent must use personal initiative to identify and solicit sales prospects. Few agents can survive in the insurance field by relying solely on contacts made through regular business and social channels. They must make active client solicitation a part of their regular job. One company, for example, asks that each agent make between 20 and 30 personal contacts with prospective customers each week, through which eight to 12 interviews may be obtained, resulting in from zero to three sales. As in many sales occupations, many days or weeks may pass without any sales, and then several sales in a row may suddenly develop.

Some agents obtain leads for sales prospects by following newspaper reports to learn of newcomers to the community, births, graduations, and business promotions. Other agents specialize in occupational groups, selling to physicians, farmers, or small businesses. Many agents use general telephone or mail solicitations to help identify prospects. All agents hope that satisfied customers will suggest future sales to their friends and neighbors.

Successful contact with prospective clients may be a difficult process. Many potential customers already may have been solicited by a number of insurance agents or may not be interested in buying insurance at a particular time. Agents are often hard-pressed to obtain their initial goal—a personal interview to sit down and talk about insurance with the potential customer.

Once they have lined up a sales interview, agents usually travel to the customer's home or place of business. During this meeting, agents explain their services. Like any other successful sales pitch, this explanation must be adapted to the needs of the client. For example, a new father may wish to ensure his child's college education, while an older person may be most interested in provisions dealing with retirement income. Or a company may be seeking protection for its new industrial plant and its related business activities. With experience, agents learn how best to answer questions or objections raised by potential customers. The agents must be able to describe the coverage offered by their company in clear, nontechnical language.

With the approval of the prospective client, the agent develops an insurance plan. To best satisfy the customer's insurance needs, and in keeping with the customer's ability to pay, the agent may present a variety of insurance options. When a life insurance policy is needed, for example, the agent may recommend term insurance (the cheapest form of insurance since it may only be used as a death benefit) or ordinary life (which may be maintained by premium payments throughout the insured's life but may be converted to aid in retirement living). In some cases, the agent may suggest a limited payment plan, such as 20-payment life, which allows the insured to pay the policy off completely in a given number of annual premiums. The agent's skill and the variety of plans offered by the company are combined to develop the best possible insurance proposal for customers.

Closing the transaction is probably the most difficult part of the insurance process. At this point, the customer must decide whether to purchase the recommended insurance plan, ask for a modified version, or conclude that additional insurance is not needed or affordable.

After a customer decides to purchase a policy, the agent must arrange for the house or other type of property to be appraised or, if a health insurance policy is being purchased, ask the customer to take a physical examination (insurance company policies require that standard rates apply only to those people in good health). The agent also must obtain a completed insurance application and the first premium payment and send them with other supporting documents to the company for its approval and formal issuance of the policy.

The final phase of the insurance process is follow up. The agent checks back frequently with policyholders both to provide service and to watch for opportunities for additional sales.

Successful insurance agents and brokers work hard at their jobs. Because arranging a meeting often means fitting into the client's personal schedule, many of the hours worked by insurance agents are in the evenings or on weekends. In addition to the time spent with customers, agents must spend time in their homes or offices preparing insurance programs for customer approval, developing new sources of business, and writing reports for the company.

REQUIREMENTS

High School

Formal requirements for the insurance field are few. Because more mature individuals are usually better able to master the complexities of the business and inspire customer confidence, most companies prefer to hire people who are at least 21 years of age. Many starting agents are more than 30 years of age. If this field interests you, there are a number of courses you can take in high school to prepare yourself for college and this type of work. Naturally you should take English classes. These classes will help you improve your research, writing, and possibly speaking skills—all communication skills that you will use in this line of work. (Taking a foreign language such as Spanish is also a good idea if you plan to work with customers who do not speak English as a first language.) Business classes will teach you how to interact professionally with others and deal with customer needs. If your high school offers economics or finance classes, take these as well. Working with insurance means working with money and numbers, and these classes will give you this exposure. You may also benefit from taking sociology and psychology classes, which can give you a greater understanding of people. Finally, take math and computer classes. Undoubtedly you will be using computers in your professional life, so start becoming comfortable with this tool now.

Postsecondary Training

Today most insurance companies and agencies prefer to hire college graduates. Those who have majored in economics or business will likely have an advantage in getting jobs. Classes you can take in college that will help you in this field include math, economics, and accounting. Business law, government, and business administration classes will help you understand the functions of different types of insurance as well as learn how to successfully run a business. Of course, keep up with your computer education. Knowing how to use software, such as spreadsheet software, will be indispensable in your line of work. You may want to attend a college or university that offers specific courses in insurance; there are many colleges and universities in the United States that offer such classes. A few schools offer bachelor's degrees in insurance.

Certification or Licensing
For full professional status, many companies recommend that their life insurance or health insurance agents become chartered life underwriters, registered health underwriters, and/or chartered financial consultants. To earn these designations, agents must successfully complete at least three years of work in the field and course work offered through the American College. This work will demonstrate the agents' ability to apply their knowledge of life insurance fundamentals, economics, business law, taxation, trusts, and finance to common insurance problems.

Those property and casualty insurance agents who wish to seek the highest professional status may pursue the designation of chartered property casualty underwriter (CPCU). To earn the designation, agents must complete at least three years in the field successfully, demonstrate high ethical practices in all work, and pass a series of examinations offered by the American Institute for Chartered Property and Casualty Underwriters (AICPCU). Agents and brokers may prepare for these examinations through home study or by taking courses offered by colleges, insurance associations, or individual companies. The AICPCU also offers an eight-exam CPCU program that allows agents to specialize in either personal or commercial insurance.

Additionally, the Independent Insurance Agents and Brokers of America offers several general certification designations to agents who are new to the field or who are interested in improving their sales skills. The AICPCU offers a certification program in general insurance as well. The National Alliance for Insurance Education and Research (http://www.scic.com) offers the certified insurance counselor and certified insurance service representative designations to agents and brokers who complete short seminars about issues in the field. Contact the alliance for more information.

Insurance agents must obtain a license in each state in which they sell insurance. There are separate licenses for each type of major insurance specialty. Agents are often sponsored for this license by the company they represent, which usually pays the license fee.

In most states, before a license is issued, the agent must pass a written test on insurance fundamentals and state insurance laws. Companies usually provide training programs to help prepare for these examinations. Often, the new agent may sell on a temporary certificate while preparing for the written examination. Information on state insurance licensing requirements can be easily obtained from the state commissioner of insurance. Agents who sell securities, such as mutual funds, must obtain a separate securities license.

Other Requirements
Personal characteristics of agents are of great importance. The following traits are most helpful: a genuine liking and appreciation for people; a positive attitude toward others and sympathy for their problems; a personal belief in the value of insurance coverage; a willingness to spend several years learning the business and becoming established; and persistence, hard work, and patience. Sales workers should also be resourceful and organized to make the most effective use of their time.

Requirements for success in insurance are elusive, and it is this fact that contributes to the high turnover rate in this field. Despite the high rate of failure, insurance sales offers a rewarding career for those who meet its requirements. It has been said that life insurance offers the easiest way to earn $1,000 to $2,000 a week, but the most difficult way to earn $300 or $400. People with strong qualifications may readily develop a successful insurance career, but poorly qualified people will find it a very difficult field.

EXPLORING

Because of state licensing requirements, it is difficult for young people to obtain actual experience. The most notable exceptions are the student-agency programs developed by several insurance companies to provide college students with practical sales experience and a trial exposure to the field.

To get a general idea of how business transactions take place in the professional world, join or start a business club at your school. You might also be able to get a part-time or summer job as a clerical worker in an insurance agency. This work will provide background information on the requirements for the field and an understanding of its problems and prospects for the future. Formal college or evening school courses in insurance will also provide a clearer picture of this profession's techniques and opportunities.

EMPLOYERS

Insurance agents and brokers are employed throughout the country, but most work in or near large cities. The majority work out of local offices or in independent agencies or brokerages; others are employed at insurance company headquarters. There are approximately 436,000 insurance agents and brokers working in the United States. Approximately 26 percent of insurance sales agents are self-employed.

STARTING OUT

Aspiring agents may apply directly to personnel directors of insurance companies or managers of branches or agencies. In most cases, the new agent will be affiliated with a local sales office almost immediately. To increase the agency's potential sales volume, the typical insurance office manager is prepared to hire all candidates who can be readily recruited and properly trained. Prospective insurance agents should discuss their career interests with representatives of several companies to select the employer that offers them the best opportunities to fulfill their goals.

Prospective agents should carefully evaluate potential employers to select an organization that offers sound training, personal supervision, resources to assist sales, adequate financial compensation, and a recognizable name that will be well received by customers. Students graduating from college should be able to arrange campus interviews with recruiters from several insurance companies. People with sales experience in other fields usually find insurance managers eager to discuss employment opportunities.

In addition to discussing personal interests and requirements for success in the field, company representatives usually give prospective agents aptitude tests, which are developed either by their company, by LIMRA International (formerly the Life Insurance Marketing and Research Association), or other organizations.

Formal job training usually involves three phases. In precontract orientation, candidates are provided with a clearer picture of the field through classroom work, training manuals, or other materials. On-the-job training is designed to present insurance fundamentals, techniques of developing sales prospects, principles of selling, and the importance of a work schedule. Finally, intermediate instruction usually provides company training of an advanced nature.

ADVANCEMENT

Continuing education has become essential for insurance agents. Several professional organizations offer courses and tests for agents to obtain additional professional certification. Although voluntary, many professional insurance organizations require agents to commit to continuing education on a regular basis. Membership in professional organizations and the accompanying certification is important in establishing client trust. Many states also require continuing education to maintain licensing.

Unlike some occupations, many of the ablest people in the insurance field are not interested in advancing into management. There can be many reasons for this. In some cases, a successful sales agent may be able to earn more than the president of the company. Experienced agents often would rather increase their volume of business and quality of service rather than their responsibility for the work of others. Others develop by specializing in various phases of insurance.

Still, many successful agents aspire to positions in sales management. At first, they may begin by helping train newcomers to the field. Later, they may become assistant managers of their office. Top agents are often asked by their companies (or even by rival insurance companies) to take over as managers of an existing branch or to develop a new one. In some cases, persons entering management must take a temporary salary cut, particularly at the beginning, and may earn less than successful agents.

There are several types of insurance sales office arrangements. *Branch office managers* are salaried employees who work for their company in a geographic region. *General agency managers* are given franchises by a company and develop and finance their own sales office. *General agents* are not directly affiliated with their company, but they must operate in a responsible manner to maintain their right to represent the company. *General insurance brokers* are self-employed persons who place insurance coverage for their clients with more than one insurance company.

The highest management positions in the insurance field are in company headquarters. Persons with expertise in sales and field management experience may be offered a position with the home office.

EARNINGS

According to the U.S. Department of Labor, in 2007 the median yearly income of insurance agents and brokers was $44,110. The department also reported that the lowest paid 10 percent of these workers, which typically includes those just beginning in the field, made less than $25,230. The highest paid 10 percent earned $113,190 or more. Many offices also pay bonuses to agents who sell a predetermined amount of coverage. Beginning agents usually receive some form of financial assistance from the company. They may be placed on a moderate salary for a year or two; often the amount of salary declines each month on the assumption that commission income on sales will increase. Eventually, the straight salary is replaced by a drawing account—a fixed dollar amount that is advanced each month against anticipated commissions. This account helps agents balance out high- and low-earning periods.

Agents receive commissions on two levels: a first-year commission for making the sale (usually 55 percent of the total first-year premium) and a series of smaller commissions paid when the insured pays the annual premium (usually 5 percent of the yearly payments for nine years). Most companies will not pay renewal commissions to agents who resign.

Agents who work for a company usually receive benefits such as vacation days, sick leave, health and life insurance, and a savings and pension program. They may also receive reimbursement for continuing education and automobile and transportation expenses. Self-employed agents must provide their own benefits.

WORK ENVIRONMENT

The job of the insurance agent is marked by extensive contact with others. Most agents actively participate in groups such as churches, synagogues, community groups, and service clubs, through which they can meet prospective clients. Insurance agents also have to stay in touch with other individuals to keep their prospective sales list growing.

Because they are essentially self-employed, agents must be self-motivated and capable of operating on their own. In return, the insurance field offers people the chance to go into business for themselves without the need for capital investment, long-term debt, and personal liability.

When asked to comment on what they liked least about the insurance field, a group of experienced agents listed the amount of detail work required of an agent, the lack of education by the public concerning insurance, the uncertainty of earnings while becoming established in the field, and the amount of night and weekend work. The last point is particularly important. Some agents work four nights a week and both days of the weekend when starting out. After becoming established, this may be reduced to two or three evenings and only one weekend day. Agents are often torn between the desire to spend more time with their families and the reality that curtailing evening and weekend work may hurt their income. Most agents work a 40-hour week, although those beginning in the field and those with thriving businesses may work longer, some up to 60 hours.

OUTLOOK

The U.S. Department of Labor predicts that employment for insurance agents and brokers will grow about as fast as the average for all careers through 2016. The percentage of people older than 65 is growing at a much faster rate than that of the general population. Agents will be needed to meet the special needs of this group, including converting some insurance policies from a death benefit to retirement income and selling an increasing number of health insurance and long-term-care insurance policies. Also, the 25- to 54-year-old age group is growing. This is the age group that has the greatest need for insurance, and agents will be needed to provide them with services. The U.S. Department of Labor also predicts that sale of commercial insurance (such as product liability, employee benefits, workers' compensation, and pollution liability insurance) will also increase. Finally, employment opportunities for insurance agents will be aided by the general increase in the nation's population, the heavy turnover among new agents, and the openings created by agents retiring or leaving the field. Opportunities will be strongest for agents who speak a foreign language and for those who pursue continuing and advanced education.

A number of factors may limit job growth in this field. Department stores and other businesses outside the traditional insurance industry have begun to offer insurance. Also, customer service representatives are increasingly assuming some sales functions, such as expanding accounts and occasionally generating new accounts. Many companies are diversifying their marketing efforts to include some direct mail and telephone sales. Increased use of computers will lessen the workload of agents by creating a database for tailor-made policies. Rising productivity among existing agents may hold down new job openings.

FOR MORE INFORMATION

The American College is the nation's oldest distance learning institution for financial service education. For information regarding the CLU and ChFC designations, contact
    The American College
    270 South Bryn Mawr Avenue
    Bryn Mawr, PA 19010-2105
    Tel: 888-263-7265
    http://www.theamericancollege.edu

For information regarding the CPCU designation, continuing education courses, and industry news, contact
    American Institute for Chartered Property and Casualty Underwriters/Insurance Institute of America
    720 Providence Road, Suite 100
    Malvern, PA 19355-3433

Tel: 800-644-2101
Email: customerservice@cpcuiia.org
http://www.aicpcu.org

For information on scholarships and opportunities for women in the insurance industry, contact
Association of Professional Insurance Women
555 Fifth Avenue, 8th Floor
New York, NY 10017-2416
Tel: 212-867-0228
http://www.apiw.org

The IIABA is the nation's oldest and largest independent agent and broker association and offers certification, job, and consumer information.
Independent Insurance Agents and Brokers of America (IIABA)
127 South Peyton Street
Alexandria, VA 22314-2879
Tel: 800-221-7917
Email: info@iiaba.org
http://www.iiaba.net

For information on educational programs, contact
Insurance Educational Association
2670 North Main Street, Suite 350
Santa Ana, CA 92705-6648
Tel: 800-655-4432
Email: info@ieatraining.com
http://www.ieatraining.com

For general information about the insurance industry, contact
Insurance Information Institute
110 William Street
New York, NY 10038-3901
Tel: 212-346-5500
http://www.iii.org

For information on insurance careers and scholarships, contact
Insurance Vocational Education Student Training
127 South Peyton Street
Alexandria, VA 22314-2879
Tel: 800-221-7917
Email: info@investprogram.org
http://www.investprogram.org

The following organization represents independent professional insurance agents. Visit its Web site for more information.
National Association of Professional Insurance Agents
400 North Washington Street
Alexandria, VA 22314-2312
Tel: 703-836-9340
http://www.pianet.org

For information on insurance aptitude tests, contact
LIMRA International
300 Day Hill Road
Windsor, CT 06095-1783
Tel: 860-285-7789
http://www.limra.com

For industry information, contact
National Association of Health Underwriters
2000 North 14th Street, Suite 450
Arlington, VA 22201-2573
Tel: 703-276-0220
Email: info@nahu.org
http://www.nahu.org

For information on continuing education, contact
National Association of Insurance and Financial Advisors
2901 Telestar Court
PO Box 12012
Falls Church, VA 22042-1205
Tel: 877-866-2432
http://www.naifa.org

This society is a professional organization consisting of graduates from The American College and other professionals in the insurance and finance fields.
Society of Financial Service Professionals
17 Campus Boulevard, Suite 201
Newtown Square, PA 19073-3230
Tel: 610-526-2500
http://www.financialpro.org

For information on insurance careers in Canada, contact
Insurance Institute of Canada
18 King Street East, 16th Floor
Toronto, ON M5C 1C4 Canada

Tel: 416-362-8586
http://www.iic-iac.org

INTERVIEW

Marty Kopach is a financial representative for Northwestern Mutual Financial Network. He discussed his career with the editors of Careers in Focus: Sales.

Q. Tell us about yourself and your business.
A. I am in business to provide financial solutions to individuals regarding their life and disability insurance needs, their retirement needs, their college education needs, and asset transfer needs. The products used are mutual funds, exchange traded funds, life insurance, and disability insurance. We are an independent small business with one to two employees.

Q. What is your work environment like?
A. Unlike many corporate jobs, my work environment is very independent. Our job is broken down into two main areas: 1) sales and personal service, which consists of face to face meetings with current and potential clients; and, 2) back office service, which consists of paperwork, service calls from clients, and product management. I am solely responsible for the sales work, and I oversee the back office work, but that is mainly handled by my staff.

Q. What is one thing that young people may not know about your career?
A. Doing planning isn't as much numbers as it is dealing with people and their emotions. Certainly there is a certain amount of analytical training required, but the ability to sit down with somebody and get them to take action on something they need to do but don't necessarily want to do is such an essential skill in this business.

Q. How did you train for this job?
A. I was an accounting major in college and passed the CPA exam. Most of my training was accounting/finance related. That created a major uphill battle for me starting in this career. I had no sales experience. It took me a good two years to get a handle on what sales really was.

Q. What are some of the pros and cons of your job?
A. The pros of the job: Freedom to make your own schedule, work with who you want to work with, unlimited income potential. The cons: Hearing "No" all the time and unlimited income potential comes with no guarantees.

Q. What are the most important personal and professional qualities for people in your career?
A. Honesty and persistence are essential to the career. There are plenty of planners with every credential out there who do a disservice to their clients.

Q. What advice would you give to young people who are interested in the field?
A. My advice for anyone interested in the field is to try it ASAP. The worst outcome would be leaving after a year or more and having an invaluable sales experience. No book or class can teach what it is like to sit in front of an individual and make a recommendation on what is best for him or her and to see that recommendation through. Any successful career takes some salesmanship, and this is the easiest way to get a chance to learn that.

Internet Store Managers and Entrepreneurs

QUICK FACTS

School Subjects
Business
Computer science

Personal Skills
Leadership/management
Technical/scientific

Work Environment
Primarily indoors
Primarily one location

Minimum Education Level
Bachelor's degree

Salary Range
$0 to $25,000 to $125,000+

Certification or Licensing
Voluntary (certification)
Required by certain states (licensing)

Outlook
Faster than the average

DOT
N/A

GOE
N/A

NOC
N/A

O*NET-SOC
N/A

OVERVIEW

Internet store managers and entrepreneurs use the exciting technology of the Internet to sell products or services. They may research the marketability of a product or service, decide on what product or service to sell, organize their business, and set up their storefront on the Web. Numerous small business owners who sell a limited number of products or a specific service have found the Internet a great place to begin their business venture because start-up costs may be less than for traditional businesses. Internet entrepreneurs run their own businesses. Internet store managers are employed by Internet entrepreneurs and stores.

HISTORY

The Internet became a popular sales tool in the 1990s, and continues to grow today. Although many dot-com companies failed in the early 2000s, Internet sales remain an integral part of our economy. Online sales managers have been listed on *U.S. News & World Report*'s Top 20 Hot Job Tracks.

In 2002, lawmakers and tax officials from 30 states agreed to enter a voluntary pact to collect online sales tax. According to Washingtonpost.com, this action was taken partially in response to regular "bricks-and-mortar" stores who complained that online retailers had an advantage.

More and more revenue is generated online each year, and some Internet stores, such as Amazon.com, have had tremendous success in this field. As the Internet continues to grow in popularity and importance, more consumers will be exposed to Internet stores on a daily basis. This will create a strong demand for Internet managers and entrepreneurs to research and market potential products and services, as well as manage businesses and employees.

THE JOB

In spite of the failure of many high-profile dot-coms in the early 2000s, many online businesses have continued to survive and thrive. These e-tailers have adapted to the constantly changing technology, economic climate, business trends, and consumer demands, instead of concentrating on fast growth and offering the lowest prices. Reports by research firm Jupiter Communications show that consumers are using Internet stores to do comparison shopping, and a significant number of consumers research products online before buying them at traditional stores.

Because of the vastness of the Internet, the role of an Internet store manager or entrepreneur can vary as much as the numerous Web sites on the Internet. Expert opinion on what makes one Web site or one business more successful than another differs, too. E-commerce is a new and relatively unexplored field for entrepreneurs. But, because most entrepreneurs have innovative and creative natures, this uncertainty and uncharted territory is what they love.

Like traditional entrepreneurs, Internet entrepreneurs must have strong business skills. They come up with ideas for an Internet product or service, research the feasibility of selling this product or service, decide what they need to charge to make a profit, determine how to advertise their business, and even arrange for financing for their business if necessary. In addition, Internet entrepreneurs typically have computer savvy and may even create and maintain their own sites.

Some entrepreneurs may choose to market a service, such as Web site design, to target the business-to-business market. Other Internet entrepreneurs may decide to market a service, such as computer dating, to target the individual consumer market. Still others may develop a "virtual store" on the Internet and sell products that target businesses or individual consumers.

Internet stores vary in size, items for sale, and the range of products. Smaller Internet stores, for example, may market the work done by a single craftsperson or businessperson. Many large Internet stores focus on selling a specific product or line of products. As some of these stores have grown they have diversified their merchandise. Amazon.com is one such example. Originally a small, online bookstore, the company now sells music CDs, videos, jewelry, toys and housewares, along with books. Other Internet stores, such as those of Eddie Bauer and Sears, may be extensions of catalog or traditional brick-and-mortar stores. These large companies are generally so well established that they can employ Internet store managers to oversee the virtual store.

Many Internet businesses begin small, with one person working as the owner, manager, Webmaster, marketing director, and accountant, among other positions. John Axne of Chicago, Illinois, took on all these responsibilities when he developed his own one-person business designing Web sites for small companies and corporations. "Having my own business allows me more creative freedom," says Axne. The successful Internet entrepreneur, like the successful traditional entrepreneur, is often able to combine his or her interests with work to fill a niche in the business world. "It's a great fit for me," Axne explains. "I have a passion for computers and a love of learning. This business allows me to sell myself and my services." Dave Wright of Venice, California, is also an Internet entrepreneur and Web site designer. He, too, combined his interests with computer skills to start his business. "I had a strong interest in art," he says. "I simply married my art and graphic art experience with computers."

Those who want to start their own businesses on the Web must be very focused and self-motivated. Just like any other entrepreneur, they always need to keep an eye on the competition to see what products and services as well as prices and delivery times others offer. While Internet entrepreneurs do not need to be computer whizzes, they should enjoy learning about technology so that they can keep up with new developments that may help them with their businesses. Internet entrepreneurs must also be decision makers, and many are drawn to running their own businesses because of the control it offers. "I'm a control freak," Wright admits. "This way I can oversee every aspect of my job."

The typical day of the Internet store manager or entrepreneur will depend greatly on the company he or she works for. Someone who works for a large company that also has a Web site store, for example, may meet with company department heads to find out about upcoming sales or products that should be heavily advertised on the Web site. They may do research about the store use and report their findings to company managers. They may work on the site itself, updating it with new information.

The Internet entrepreneur also has varied responsibilities that depend on his or her business. Wright notes, "No two projects and no two days are alike." An entrepreneur may spend one day working with a client to determine the client's needs and the next day working on bookkeeping and advertising in addition to working on a project. Most entrepreneurs, however, enjoy this variety and flexibility.

While the Internet world is appealing to many, there are risks for those who start their own businesses. "The Internet changes so rapidly that in five years it may be entirely different," Wright says. "That's why I started a business that simply sells services and didn't require a major investment. It is a business that I can get into and out of quickly if I find it necessary. There is no product, per se, and no inventory." Despite uncertainties, however, Web stores continue to open and the number of Internet store managers and entrepreneurs continues to grow.

REQUIREMENTS

High School

If you are considering becoming an Internet store manager or entrepreneur, there are a number of classes you can take in high school to help prepare you for these careers. Naturally you should take computer science courses to give you a familiarity with using computers and the Web. Business and marketing courses will also be beneficial. Also, take mathematics, accounting, or bookkeeping classes because, as an entrepreneur, you will be responsible for your company's finances. Take history classes to learn about economic trends and psychology classes to learn about human behavior. A lot of advertising and product promotion has a psychological element. Finally, take plenty of English classes. These classes will help you develop your communication skills—skills that will be vital to your work as a store manager or business owner.

Postsecondary Training

Although there are no specific educational requirements for Internet store managers or entrepreneurs, a college education will certainly enhance your skills and chances for success. Like anyone interested in working for or running a traditional business, take plenty of business, economics, and marketing and management classes. Your education should also include accounting or bookkeeping classes. Keep up with computer and Internet developments by taking computer classes. Some schools offer certificates and degrees in e-commerce. Many schools have undergraduate degree programs in business or business administration, but you can also enter this field with other degrees. Dave Wright, for example, graduated with a degree from art school, while John Axne has degrees in biomedical engineering and interactive media.

Certification or Licensing
While there are no specific certifications available for Internet store managers and entrepreneurs, professional associations such as the Institute for Certification of Computing Professionals and the Institute of Certified Professional Managers offer voluntary management-related certifications to industry professionals. These designations are helpful in proving your abilities to an employer. The more certifications you have, the more you have to offer.

Licenses may be required for running a business, depending on the type of business. Since requirements vary, you will need to check with local and state agencies for regulations in your area.

Other Requirements
Internet entrepreneurs and store managers must have the desire and initiative to keep up on new technology and business trends. Because they must deal with many different people in various lines of work, they need to be flexible problem solvers and have strong communication skills. Creativity and insight into new and different ways of doing business are qualities that are essential for an entrepreneur to be successful. In addition, because the Internet and e-commerce are relatively new and the future of Internet businesses is uncertain, those who enter the field are generally risk-takers and eager to be on the cutting edge of commerce and technology. Dave Wright notes, "This is not a job for someone looking for security. The Internet world is always changing. This is both exciting and scary to me as a businessperson. This is one career where you are not able to see where you will be in five years."

EXPLORING
There are numerous ways in which you can explore your interest in the computer and business worlds. Increase your computer skills and find out how much this technology interests you by joining a computer users group or club at your high school or your community. Access the Internet frequently on your own to observe different Web site designs and find out what is being sold and marketed electronically. What sites do you think are best at promoting products and why? Think about things from a customer's point of view. How easy are the sites

Most Popular Online Retailers

1. Amazon.com
2. eBay.com
3. Wal-Mart.com
4. BestBuy.com
5. JCPenney.com
6. Target.com
7. Google.com
8. Overstock.com
9. Kohls.com
10. Sears.com

Source: *STORES*, October 2008

---

to access and use? How are the products displayed and accessed? How competitive are the prices for goods or services?

Make it a goal to come up with your own ideas for a product or service to market on the Web, then do some research. How difficult would it be to deliver the product? What type of financing would be involved? Are there other sites already providing this product or service? How could you make your business unique?

Talk to professionals in your community about their work. Set up information interviews with local business owners to find out what is involved in starting and running a traditional business. Your local chamber of commerce or the Small Business Administration may have classes or publications that would help you learn about starting a business. In addition, set up information interviews with computer consultants, Web site designers, or Internet store managers or owners. How did they get started? What advice do they have? Is there anything they wish they had done differently? Where do they see the future of e-commerce going?

If your school has a future business owners club, join this group to meet others with similar interests. For hands-on business experience, get a part-time or summer job at any type of store in your area. This work will give you the opportunity to deal with customers (who can sometimes be hard to please), work with handling money, and observe how the store promotes its products and services.

EMPLOYERS

Internet store managers may work for an established traditional business or institution that also has a Web site dealing with products and services. The manager may also work for a business that only has a presence on the Web or for an Internet entrepreneur. Entrepreneurs are self-employed, and sometimes they may employ people to work under them. Some Internet entrepreneurs may be hired to begin a business for someone else.

STARTING OUT

Professionals in the field advise those just starting out to work for someone else to gain experience in the business world before beginning their own business. The Internet is a good resource to use to find employment. There are many sites that post job openings. Local employment agencies and newspapers and trade magazines also list job opportunities. In addition, your college career services office should be able to provide you with help locating a job. Networking with college alumni and people in your computer users groups may also provide job leads.

ADVANCEMENT

Advancement opportunities depend on the business, its success, and the individual's goals. Internet entrepreneurs or store managers who are successful may enter other business fields or consulting. Or they may advance to higher-level management positions or other larger Internet-based businesses. Some entrepreneurs establish a business and then sell it only to begin another business venture. The Internet world is constantly changing because of technological advancements. This state of flux means that a wide variety of possibilities are available to those working in the field. "There is no solid career path in the Internet field," says Dave Wright. "Your next career may not even be developed yet."

EARNINGS

Income for Internet store managers and entrepreneurs is usually tied to the profitability of the business. Internet store managers who work for established traditional businesses are typically salaried employees of the company. Internet entrepreneurs who offer a service may be paid by the project. Entrepreneurs are self-employed and their income will depend on the success of the business. Those just starting out may actually have no earnings, while those with a business that has been in existence for several years may have annual earnings between $25,000 and $50,000. Some in the field may earn much more than this amount. John Axne estimates that those who have good technical skills and can do such things as create the database program for a Web site may have higher salaries, in the $60,000 to $125,000 range.

Entrepreneurs are almost always responsible for their own medical, disability, and life insurances. Retirement plans must also be self-funded and self-directed. Internet store managers may or may not receive benefits.

WORK ENVIRONMENT

Internet entrepreneurs and store managers may work out of a home or private office. Some Internet store managers may be required to work on site at a corporation or small business.

The entrepreneur must deal with the stresses of starting a business, keeping it going, dealing with deadlines and customers, and coping with problems as they arise. They must also work long hours to develop and manage their business venture; many entrepreneurs work over 40 hours a week. Evening or weekend work may also be required, both for the entrepreneur and the store manager.

In addition, these professionals must spend time researching, reading, and checking out the competition in order to be informed about the latest technology and business trends. Their intensive computer work can result in eyestrain, hand and wrist injuries, and back pain.

OUTLOOK

Online commerce is a new and exciting field with tremendous potential, and it is likely that growth will continue over the long term. However, it is important to keep in mind that the failure rate for new businesses, even traditional ones, is fairly high. Some experts predict that in the next few years, 80 to 90 percent of dot-coms will either close or be acquired by other companies. The survivors will be small businesses that are able to find niche markets, anticipate trends, adapt to market and technology changes, and plan for a large enough financial margin to turn a profit. Analysts also anticipate that the amount of business-to-business e-commerce will surpass business-to-consumer sales.

Internet managers and entrepreneurs with the most thorough education and experience and who have done their research will have the best opportunities for success. For those who are adventurous

102 Careers in Focus: Sales

and interested in using new avenues for selling products and services, the Internet offers many possibilities.

FOR MORE INFORMATION

For information about the information technology industry and e-commerce, contact
 Information Technology Association of America
 1401 Wilson Boulevard, Suite 1100
 Arlington, VA 22209-2318
 Tel: 703-522-5055
 http://www.itaa.org

For information on certification, contact
 Institute for Certification of Computing Professionals
 2350 East Devon Avenue, Suite 115
 Des Plaines, IL 60018-4610
 Tel: 800-843-8227
 http://www.iccp.org

For information on certification, contact
 Institute of Certified Professional Managers
 James Madison University
 MSC 5504
 Harrisonburg, VA 22807-0001
 Tel: 800-568-4120
 http://icpm.biz

The Small Business Administration offers helpful information on starting a business. For information on state offices and additional references, visit its Web site.
 Small Business Administration
 409 Third Street, SW
 Washington, DC 20416-0001
 Tel: 800-827-5722
 Email: answerdesk@sba.gov
 http://www.sba.gov

Check out the following online magazine specializing in topics of interest to entrepreneurs:
 Entrepreneur.com
 http://www.entrepreneur.com

Internet Transaction Specialists

OVERVIEW

Depending on their level of expertise, *Internet transaction specialists* may be in charge of designing, developing, or implementing Internet transaction software or systems. This software or system is the technology that allows a customer to buy a book online, for example, by giving his or her credit card number. Internet transaction specialists at the most advanced professional level are often called *architects,* and they oversee the design of the whole transaction system. They decide what direction a system should take and what technology should be used. *Software developers* work under the guidance of architects to turn these designs into reality. Less experienced programmers may also contribute by working on smaller parts of the program that the developer or architect assigns them.

HISTORY

Since the boom of the World Wide Web in the 1990s, companies have flocked to use Internet technology to communicate with employees, customers, clients, buyers, and future stockholders. As a result, these companies need workers to ensure that their systems are secure, and to develop improved systems so that transactions can take place more quickly.

At first, the majority of Internet sites were created and maintained by a sole individual who was a jack-of-all-trades. Today, Web sites are often designed, implemented, and managed by entire departments composed of numerous individuals, such as Internet transaction

---

QUICK FACTS

School Subjects
Business
Computer science
Mathematics

Personal Skills
Communication/ideas
Technical/scientific

Work Environment
Primarily indoors
Primarily one location

Minimum Education Level
Bachelor's degree

Salary Range
$37,600 to $83,130 to $125,260+

Certification or Licensing
Voluntary

Outlook
Faster than the average

DOT
N/A

GOE
N/A

NOC
N/A

O*NET-SOC
15-1031.00, 15-1099.02

specialists, who specialize in creating the systems or software used to conduct transactions on the Internet.

As consumers become more comfortable with buying online and companies expand their Internet businesses, Internet transaction specialists will be needed to ensure that systems run smoothly and efficiently.

THE JOB

Every business engaged in e-commerce must use some type of Internet transaction software, that is, software that allows money to be transferred from the customer to the business. This process is also referred to as *electronic funds transfer (EFT)*. Transaction software and systems are what allow customers to do such things as transfer funds between banks, pay bills online, and buy and sell stocks. At the same time, transaction software and systems are what allow businesses to get credit card approval for a customer's purchase, receive payments, and make money transfers. As e-commerce has become more and more popular, the need for Internet transaction specialists has grown. In addition, the technology itself continues to develop. According to Gene Krause, president and director of sales and marketing of Intellefunds, Inc., in St. Louis, Missouri, "Electronic funds transfer is continually evolving. It is getting better and more efficient and is revolutionizing Internet transactions."

One of the major responsibilities of an Internet transaction specialist is to ensure the security of a system. Because these transactions involve money and because they take place over the Internet, the possibility exists for online robbery or "cybercrime." Customers need to feel sure that when they buy shoes or groceries online, for example, their credit card numbers won't be stolen or their bank accounts emptied by hackers breaking into the system. Transaction specialists constantly work to improve protocols for secure financial transactions. Jeff Thorness, of ACH Direct in Allen, Texas, an EFT company, is his company's primary programmer as well as chief executive officer. Security is one of his top concerns. "Our software is very sophisticated and secure," he explains. "We can quickly deal with problems where the purchase may be over the credit limit or where fraud is suspected. Our software can analyze transactions immediately."

Another major responsibility of the specialist is to improve software and systems so that transactions are speedier and less complicated, allowing banks, credit card companies, and stores selling goods online to exchange financial data more rapidly and directly than ever before. Improvements also provide customers greater access to goods and services. Through EFT, for example, customers may be able to transfer funds from a bank account directly to a business. Thorness explains, "Electronic funds transfer even allows the consumer who has no credit cards to purchase products online." He says that this is also good for the business because, "It enables a larger Internet client base."

Some companies have large enough e-commerce needs that they have their own in-house Internet architects, developers, and programmers designing and implementing transaction systems. Other smaller companies may hire a firm specializing in e-commerce systems to perform this service. Some firms specializing in transaction software simply implement that software for companies developing or improving their e-commerce sites. On the cutting edge are firms working to push transaction software standards forward, developing new ways to perform transactions online.

Thorness is an in-house specialist and his days include a variety of activities. "On any given day, I may oversee the mechanical applications of the software and Web site, support the reseller, solve technical problems, and deal with customer service issues. Plus," he adds, "I must oversee the total operations side where we receive transactions that flow through our system to the Federal Reserve System." In-house specialists, as well as outside specialists who are hired by a company to work on a project, must have excellent communication skills. They meet with management to find out what services the company wants to offer its customers through the Internet and determine what type of programming is needed. Often the specialists will work with other programmers to build the software and system. In addition, specialists must be able to deal with the frustration that comes when programming does not work as they had anticipated. Tight deadlines can also make the job of the transaction specialist fairly stressful.

Despite the stress and frustration that are part of this work, many people find this job rewarding. "When you develop programs you get a sense of accomplishment throughout the job. You are actually building a product or service," Thorness says. He also sees a bright future for transaction specialists. "There are lots of career opportunities on various levels," Thorness notes. "We are in the midst of a computer revolution. Business people are talking to each other in similar languages. Transactions such as billing and bill payment over the Internet are just beginning."

REQUIREMENTS

High School

There are a number of classes you can take in high school to help get ready for this career. Improving your computer skills should be a priority; therefore, take as many computer classes as possible. Develop your analytical and problem-solving skills by taking mathematics classes such as algebra, geometry, and precalculus, and science classes, such as chemistry and physics. To get an idea of how companies function, take business and economics classes. English classes are essential and will help you develop your communication, research, and writing skills.

Postsecondary Training
In the early days of Internet and computer development, many people without college degrees were able to find jobs in the field if they had computer experience. Jeff Thorness developed his computer skills at an early age. "I was one of those lucky people who grew up understanding computers," he says. "By the time I got out of high school I knew more than they could teach me in college. I was already developing, programming, and designing complex software." However, as this field has matured and the market has grown tighter, many companies now require new hires to have college degrees. In addition, a college degree may help you to advance professionally. Typically, people entering this field have degrees in computer science; some have degrees in other areas such as computer engineering, e-commerce, business, or mathematics. The most important aspect of your education, however, is to gain a thorough knowledge of computers and programming. It will be to your benefit to complete an internship or do summer work in programming at a computer company or a company with a computer/technology division. When you are deciding on a college to attend, find out if the career services office has information on such internships or jobs and will help you find one.

People working in some advanced positions, such as architect, may be required to have extensive computer and business experience as well as an undergraduate or graduate degree.

Certification or Licensing
There are numerous certifications available in programming languages, software, and network administration. Some employers may require that you have certain certifications although most employers are more interested in your skills and experience. Nevertheless, certification will enhance your professional standing and show your commitment to the field. The certification process usually involves taking a training program and passing a written exam.

Other Requirements
You should enjoy learning about new technology and be able to learn on your own as well as through organized classes. People in

this field constantly improve their skills by reading about the latest developments and teaching themselves new techniques. You'll need the desire and initiative to keep up on new technology, software, and hardware. You must also have good verbal and written communication skills because you will often have to communicate with a team or with the end user.

Jeff Thorness states, "You must be a logical thinker and a hard worker. You must be able to concentrate for long periods of time and be persistent in finding a problem and finishing a project." You must be able to work under stressful situations, such as meeting important deadlines, and deal with frustration when the programming is not working the way you had planned. Because you will deal with many different problems you must be flexible and patient.

Depending on what area you want to specialize in, you may need good customer service skills or design ability. "If you are getting into the tech support area," Thorness says, "you must analyze and dissect the problem and have the ability to deal with all issues. You need to be helpful and have good customer service skills." He adds, "If you want to get into the Web design aspect you should have database and design skills. Again, the ability to think logically is important."

EXPLORING

One of the best ways to explore this field is to get hands-on experience working with computers. "Get a job at a computer store and get 'hands-on dirty' with the hardware issues," suggests Jeff Thorness. "Get real-world experience by getting into programming. Buy books and experiment with Web development tools." Join your high school computer users group or start one of your own. You may be able to learn about new technology developments from others in your group.

In addition to reading books on programming, look at computer magazines for the latest news. Some publications, such as the quarterly magazine *2600* (http://www.2600.com), have articles about security issues. While *2600* is aimed at hackers, reading the articles will give you an understanding of how some systems are broken into and help you develop your ability to think of defenses.

Naturally, you should use computers and the Web as often as you can. If a community center or tech school in your area offers computer classes that are more advanced than those offered at your high school, be sure to take them. Also, your computer teacher or school guidance counselor may be able to help you contact professionals in the field and set up information interviews with them. Even if you can't find an Internet transaction specialist to interview, talking with anyone in the field, such as programmers, Web site designers, or consultants, will give you an idea of what computer work is like.

EMPLOYERS

Internet transaction specialists may work in-house, as salaried employees of companies such as those with an Internet presence, those that develop software and provide electronic funds transfer services, or financial institutions. Others may work for firms that specialize in developing the transaction software and systems for companies without an in-house transaction staff. These companies hire the firms to build or improve their Internet sites.

Job opportunities are available worldwide; however, major cities with a high concentration of Internet, technology, and software companies may provide the best opportunities.

STARTING OUT

Many transaction specialists begin their careers working as junior programmers under the supervision of more experienced developers and architects. Only after they prove their skills and work ethic on the job are beginning programmers considered for positions with greater responsibility.

Apply for employment directly to consulting firms, Internet and software companies, as well as corporations, businesses, and financial institutions that have in-house computer divisions. Classified ads, employment agencies, and Internet job listings can also provide some possible job leads. Your college career services office should also be able to help you locate a position. Networking with others in the computer industry and the community is a good way to make the contacts that may lead to employment. To network, get in touch with previous business associates, computer user groups, and trade organizations. In addition, your college internship or summer work with computers may provide you with contacts and job leads. A willingness to learn and to work hard is the key to a good start as well as advancement in the computer industry.

ADVANCEMENT

Specialists who have advanced through the ranks of junior programmers to senior architects can take their careers in any of a number of directions. Those with project management skills may move up to executive managerial or supervisory positions that require more planning than programming. Persons with excellent programming and development skills may become involved in more cutting-edge programming work, like developing standards for Internet transactions.

Continued learning, certifications, and degrees may provide the specialist with a competitive edge when it comes to advancing within the industry.

EARNINGS

Earnings for transaction specialists vary and depend on factors such as a person's experience, knowledge, and geographic location as well as the size of the company he or she works for. Salaries for junior programmers without much experience usually begin around $45,000 annually. On the other end of the scale, senior software architects can earn as much as $200,000, though salaries between $75,000 and $100,000 are more common. Developers and mid-range programmers tend to fall in the middle of these two—closer to one or the other depending on their years of experience and the size of the firm. According to *Computerworld*'s 2007 Salary Survey, systems architects earned average annual salaries of $107,844 (including bonuses) in 2007. The U.S. Department of Labor lists salaries of less than $37,600 to more than $125,000 in 2007 for computer software engineers specializing in applications, including programmers, and computer systems engineers, including architects.

As with other Internet-related jobs, hourly wage figures tend to be higher for programmers working as consultants.

Typical benefits for full-time employees include health, life, and disability insurance; sick leave; and vacation pay. Retirement plans may also be available, and some companies may match employees' contributions. Some companies may also offer stock-option plans. In a highly competitive market, companies may offer a sign-on bonus to a new, talented employee.

WORK ENVIRONMENT

Internet transaction specialists can generally expect to work in a clean, comfortable office environment. The office atmosphere may vary greatly depending on the company. Those working in large, traditional businesses, such as banks, will generally experience a more formal and structured environment.

The job of the transaction specialist can be frustrating and stressful, and frequently long hours are required to finish a project. Many people in the computer field often work over 40 hours a week and are required to work nights and weekends. Jeff Thorness notes that it is common for him to work 12 hours a day, six days a week.

"When we are in the middle of designing a new system and the hours become critical, it can be more," he says. In addition, Internet transaction specialists who are dedicated to keeping up with technology and the Internet community must spend a considerable amount of their free time reading, researching, and keeping abreast of computer and Internet technologies.

To guard against eyestrain, back pain, and hand and wrist injuries that can come from intensive computer work, Internet transaction specialists must use good equipment such as appropriate chairs and keyboards.

OUTLOOK

The future of transaction specialists will be closely tied to the future of e-commerce itself. In the beginnings of e-commerce, there was extremely rapid growth for a number of high-profile successful companies. During the early 2000s, however, many of these businesses failed or were taken over by other companies, and there was a wave of layoffs and firings. Studies have shown that these companies offered large discounts to attract customers and failed to plan for a large enough financial margin to turn a profit. Many smaller businesses pulled through the dot-com crisis because they concentrated on a niche market, provided products and services targeted to their specific demands, and paid careful attention to the bottom line.

Experts predict growth for dot-com businesses in the next few years, but job security with any one firm may be uncertain. Mergers, business failures, downsizing, and the ever-changing technology of this industry mean that there may be some instability regarding long-term employment with any one firm. Nevertheless, those who keep current with technology and are always willing to learn and adapt will be in high demand.

Gene Krause sees growth possibilities for the industries involving EFT. "Electronic funds transfer is continually evolving. It is getting better and more efficient. It is revolutionizing Internet transactions," he says. Krause also predicts growth in other areas, "Electronic bill payment will also increase and it will all be Internet based. Transactions will be speedier and costs will be reduced. Transactions through bank accounts will increase." The potential advantages of secure online transactions, especially increased speed and accuracy in business-to-business communications, should continue to fuel the development of this technology for years to come. Naturally, skilled transaction specialists will be needed to make these developments possible.

FOR MORE INFORMATION

This center studies Internet security problems and provides security alerts. For industry news, check out its Web site.
CERT
4500 Fifth Avenue
Pittsburgh, PA 15213-2612
Tel: 412-268-7090
Email: cert@cert.org
http://www.cert.org

For information on the industry, conferences, and seminars, contact
Computer Security Institute
600 Harrison Street
San Francisco, CA 94107-1387
Tel: 415-947-6320
Email: csi@techweb.com
http://www.gocsi.com

In addition to providing security products and services, ICSA Labs has a professional membership organization and also runs consortia groups that share research and information on current security issues.
ICSA Labs
1000 Bent Creek Boulevard, Suite 200
Mechanicsburg, PA 17050-1881
Tel: 717-790-8100
http://www.icsalabs.com

Purchasing Agents

QUICK FACTS

School Subjects
Business
Economics
Mathematics

Personal Skills
Helping/teaching
Technical/scientific

Work Environment
Primarily indoors
Primarily one location

Minimum Education Level
Bachelor's degree

Salary Range
$27,810 to $50,000 to $86,860+

Certification or Licensing
Voluntary

Outlook
Little or no change

DOT
162

GOE
13.02.02

NOC
1225

O*NET-SOC
11-3061.00, 13-1021.00, 13-1023.00

OVERVIEW

Purchasing agents work for businesses and other large organizations, such as hospitals, universities, and government agencies. They buy raw materials, machinery, supplies, and services required for the organization. They must consider cost, quality, quantity, and time of delivery. Purchasing agents hold approximately 303,000 jobs in the United States.

HISTORY

Careers in the field of purchasing are relatively new and came into real importance only in the last half of the 20th century. The first purchasing jobs emerged during the industrial revolution, when manufacturing plants and businesses became bigger. This led to the division of management jobs into various specialties, one of which was buying.

By the late 1800s, buying was considered a separate job in large businesses. Purchasing jobs were especially important in the railroad, automobile, and steel industries. The trend toward creating specialized buying jobs was reflected in the founding of professional organizations, such as the National Association of Purchasing Agents (now the Institute for Supply Management) and the American Purchasing Society. It was not until after World War II, however, with the expansion of the U.S. government and the increased complexity of business practices, that the job of purchasing agent became firmly established.

THE JOB

Purchasing agents generally work for organizations that buy at least $100,000 worth of goods a year. Their primary goal is to purchase the best quality materials for the best price. To do this, the agent must consider the exact specifications for the required items, cost, quantity discounts, freight handling or other transportation costs, and delivery time. In the past, much of this information was obtained by comparing listings in catalogs and trade journals, interviewing suppliers' representatives, keeping up with current market trends, examining sample goods, and observing demonstrations of equipment. Increasingly, information can be found through computer databases, including those found on the Internet. Sometimes agents visit plants of company suppliers. The agent is responsible for following up on orders and ensuring that goods meet the order specifications.

Most purchasing agents work in firms that have fewer than five employees in their purchasing department. In some small organizations, there is only one person responsible for making purchases. Very large firms, however, may employ as many as 100 purchasing agents, each responsible for specific types of goods. In such organizations there is usually a purchasing director or purchasing manager.

Some purchasing agents seek the advice of *purchase-price analysts,* who compile and analyze statistical data about the manufacture and cost of products. Based on this information, they can make recommendations to purchasing personnel regarding the feasibility of producing or buying certain products and suggest ways to reduce costs.

Purchasing agents often specialize in a particular product or field. For example, *procurement engineers* specialize in aircraft equipment. They establish specifications and requirements for construction, performance, and testing of equipment.

Field contractors negotiate with farmers to grow or purchase fruits, vegetables, or other crops. These agents may advise growers on methods, acreage, and supplies, and arrange for financing, transportation, or labor recruitment.

Head tobacco buyers are engaged in the purchase of tobacco on the auction warehouse floor. They advise other buyers about grades and quantities of tobacco and suggest prices.

Grain buyers manage grain elevators. They are responsible for evaluating and buying grain for resale and milling. They are concerned with the quality, market value, shipping, and storing of grain.

Grain broker-and-market operators buy and sell grain for investors through the commodities exchange. Like other brokers, they work on a commission basis.

REQUIREMENTS
High School
Most purchasing and buying positions require at least a bachelor's degree. Therefore, while in high school, take a college preparatory curriculum. Helpful subjects include English, business, mathematics, social science, and economics.

Postsecondary Training
Although it is possible to obtain an entry-level purchasing job with only a high school diploma, many employers prefer or require college graduates for the job, and the best jobs in government and at large companies go to those with a master's degree. College work should include courses in general economics, purchasing, accounting, statistics, and business management. A familiarity with computers also is desirable. Some colleges and universities offer majors in purchasing, but other business-related majors are appropriate as well.

Purchasing agents with a master's degree in business administration, public administration, engineering, technology, or finance tend to have the best jobs and highest salaries. Companies that manufacture machinery or chemicals may require a degree in engineering or a related field. A civil service examination is required for employment in government purchasing positions.

Certification or Licensing
There are no specific licenses or certification requirements imposed by law for purchasing agents. There are, however, several professional organizations to which many purchasing agents belong, including the Institute for Supply Management, the National Institute of Government Purchasing, the Association for Operations Management, and the American Purchasing Society. These organizations offer certification to applicants who meet their educational and other requirements and who pass the necessary examinations.

The Institute for Supply Management offers the accredited purchasing practitioner and certified professional in supply management designations. The National Institute of Government Purchasing and the Universal Public Purchasing Certification Council offer the certified public purchasing officer and the certified professional public buyer designations. APICS-The Association for Operations Management offers the certified supply chain professional designation. The American Purchasing Society offers the certified purchasing professional and certified professional purchasing manager designations. Although certification is not essential, it is a recognized mark of professional competence that enhances a purchasing agent's opportunities for promotion to top management positions.

Other Requirements
Purchasing agents should have calm temperaments and have confidence in their decision-making abilities. Because they work with other people, they need to be diplomatic, tactful, and cooperative. A thorough knowledge of business practices and an understanding of the needs and activities of the employer are essential, as is knowledge of the relevant markets. It also is helpful to be familiar with social and economic changes in order to predict the amounts or types of products to buy.

EXPLORING
If you are interested in becoming a purchasing agent, you can learn more about the field through a summer job in the purchasing department of a business. Even working as a stock clerk can offer some insight into the job of purchasing agent or buyer. You may also learn about the job by talking with an experienced purchasing agent or reading publications on the field such as *Purchasing* magazine (http://www.purchasing.com). Keeping abreast of economic trends, fashion styles, or other indicators may help you to predict the market for particular products. Making educated and informed predictions is a basic part of any buying job.

EMPLOYERS
There are approximately 303,000 purchasing agents (wholesale, retail, farm products, and other) currently working in the United States. They work for a wide variety of businesses, both wholesale and retail, as well as for government agencies. Employers range from small stores, where buying may be only one function of a manager's job, to multinational corporations, where a buyer may specialize in one type of item and buy in enormous quantity. Nearly every business that sells products requires someone to purchase the goods to be sold. These businesses are located nearly everywhere there is a community of people, from small towns to large cities. Of course, the larger the town or city, the more businesses and thus

more buying positions. Larger cities provide the best opportunities for higher salaries and advancement.

STARTING OUT

Students without a college degree may be able to enter the field as clerical workers and then receive on-the-job training in purchasing. A college degree, though, is required for most higher positions. College and university career services offices offer assistance to graduating students in locating jobs.

Entry into the purchasing department of a private business can be made by direct application to the company. Some purchasing agents start in another department, such as accounting, shipping, or receiving, and transfer to purchasing when an opportunity arises. Many large companies send newly hired agents through orientation programs, where they learn about goods and services, suppliers, and purchasing methods.

Another means of entering the field is through the military. Service in the Quartermaster Corps of the Army or the procurement divisions of the Navy or Air Force can provide excellent preparation either for a civilian job or a career position in the service.

ADVANCEMENT

In general, purchasing agents begin by becoming familiar with departmental procedures, such as keeping inventory records, filling out forms to initiate new purchases, checking purchase orders, and dealing with vendors. With more experience, they gain responsibility for selecting vendors and purchasing products. Agents may become junior buyers of standard catalog items, assistant buyers, or managers, perhaps with overall responsibility for purchasing, warehousing, traffic, and related functions. The top positions are head of purchasing, purchasing director, materials manager, and vice-president of purchasing. These positions include responsibilities concerning production, planning, and marketing.

Many agents advance by changing employers. Frequently an assistant purchasing agent for one firm will be hired as a purchasing agent or head of the purchasing department by another company.

EARNINGS

How much a purchasing agent earns depends on various factors, including the employer's sales volume. Mass merchandisers, such as discount or chain department stores, pay among the highest salaries.

According to 2007 U.S. Department of Labor data, earnings for purchasing agents, except wholesale, retail, and farm products ranged from less than $32,580 for the lowest paid 10 percent to more than $86,860 for the top paid 10 percent. Median salaries were $52,460. Wholesale and retail buyers (except farm products) had median earnings of $46,960 in 2007. Their salaries ranged from less than $27,810 to $86,660 or more annually. Purchasing agents and buyers of farm products had median annual earnings of $48,410 in 2007.

In addition to their salaries, buyers often receive cash bonuses based on performance and may be offered incentive plans, such as profit sharing and stock options. Most buyers receive the usual company benefits, such as vacation, sick leave, life and health insurance, and pension plans. They generally also receive an employee's discount of 10 to 20 percent on merchandise purchased for personal use.

WORK ENVIRONMENT

Working conditions for a purchasing agent are similar to those of other office employees. They usually work in rooms that are pleasant, well lighted, and clean. Work is year-round and generally steady because it is not particularly influenced by seasonal factors. Most have 40-hour workweeks, although overtime is not uncommon. In addition to regular hours, agents may have to attend meetings, read and prepare reports, visit suppliers' plants, or travel. While most work is done indoors, some agents occasionally need to inspect goods outdoors or in warehouses.

It is important for purchasing agents to have good working relations with others. They must interact closely with suppliers as well as with personnel in other departments of the company. Because of the importance of their decisions, purchasing agents sometimes work under great pressure.

OUTLOOK

Little or no employment change is expected for purchasing agents through 2016, according to the U.S. Department of Labor. Computerized purchasing methods and the increased reliance on a select number of suppliers boost the productivity of purchasing personnel and have somewhat reduced the number of new job openings. But as more and more hospitals, schools, state and local governments, and other service-related organizations turn to professional purchasing agents to help reduce costs, they will become good sources of employment. Nevertheless, most job openings will come from a need to replace workers who retire or otherwise leave their jobs.

Demand will be strongest for those with a master's degree in business administration or an undergraduate degree in purchasing. Among firms that manufacture complex machinery, chemicals, and other technical products, the demand will be for graduates with a master's degree in engineering, another field of science, or business administration. Graduates of two-year programs in purchasing or materials management should continue to find good opportunities, especially in smaller companies.

Employment for purchasing agents, farm products is expected to decline through 2016 as a result of consolidation in the agricultural industry.

FOR MORE INFORMATION

For career and certification information, contact
American Purchasing Society
PO Box 256
Aurora, IL 60507-0256
Tel: 630-859-0250
Email: propurch@propurch.com
http://www.american-purchasing.com

For information on certification, contact
APICS-The Association for Operations Management
8430 West Bryn Mawr Avenue, Suite 1000
Chicago, IL 60631-3439
Tel: 800-444-2742
Email: service@apics.org
http://www.apics.org

For career and certification information and lists of colleges with purchasing programs, contact
Institute for Supply Management
PO Box 22160
Tempe, AZ 85285-2160
Tel: 800-888-6276
http://www.ism.ws

For information on certification and purchasing careers in government, contact
National Institute of Government Purchasing
151 Spring Street
Herndon, VA 20170-5223
Tel: 800-367-6447
http://www.nigp.org

For materials on educational programs in the retail industry, contact
   National Retail Federation
   325 Seventh Street, NW, Suite 1100
   Washington, DC 20004-2808
   Tel: 800-673-4692
   http://www.nrf.com

Real Estate Agents and Brokers

QUICK FACTS

School Subjects
Business
English
Mathematics

Personal Skills
Communication/ideas
Helping/teaching

Work Environment
Primarily indoors
Primarily multiple locations

Minimum Education Level
High school diploma

Salary Range
$20,930 to $50,000 to $145,600+

Certification or Licensing
Required

Outlook
About as fast as average

DOT
250

GOE
10.03.01

NOC
6232

O*NET-SOC
41-9021.00, 41-9022.00

OVERVIEW

Real estate brokers are business people who sell, rent, or manage the property of others. *Real estate agents* are salespeople who are either self-employed or hired by brokers. Sometimes, the term agent is applied to both real estate brokers and agents. There are approximately 564,000 real estate agents and real estate brokers employed in the United States.

HISTORY

Three factors contributed to the rise of the modern real estate business: first, the general increase in the total population and in the number of pieces of real estate for sale, second, the growing percentage of people owning property, and third, the complexity of laws regarding the transfer of real estate. These factors led to the need for experienced agents, on whom both sellers and buyers increasingly rely.

Professionalization of the real estate field developed rapidly in the 20th century. In 1908, the National Association of Realtors was founded (as the National Association of Real Estate Exchanges). This huge trade group has encouraged the highest ethical standards for the field and has lobbied hard in Congress for many of the tax advantages that homeowners and property owners now enjoy.

THE JOB

The primary responsibility of real estate brokers and agents is to help clients buy, sell, rent, or lease a piece of real estate. Real estate is defined as a piece of land or property and all improvements attached to it. The property may be residential, commercial, or agricultural. When people wish to put property up for sale or rent, they contract with real estate brokers to arrange the sale and to represent them in the transaction. This contract with a broker is called a listing.

One of the main duties of brokers is to actively solicit listings for the agency. They develop leads for potential listings by distributing promotional items, by advertising in local publications, and by showing other available properties in open houses. They also spend a great deal of time on the phone exploring leads gathered from various sources, including personal contacts.

Once a listing is obtained, real estate agents analyze the property to present it in the best possible light to prospective buyers. They have to recognize and promote the property's strong selling points. A residential real estate agent might emphasize such attributes as a home's layout or proximity to schools, for example. Agents develop descriptions to be used with photographs of the property in ads and promotions. To make a piece of real estate more attractive to prospective buyers, agents may also advise homeowners on ways to improve the look of their property to be sold.

Agents are also responsible for determining the fair market value for each property up for sale. They compare their client's real estate with similar properties in the area that have recently been sold to decide upon a fair asking price. The broker and any agents of the brokerage work to obtain the highest bid for a property because their earnings are dependent on the sale price. Owners usually sign a contract agreeing that if their property is sold, they will pay the agent a percentage of the selling price.

When the property is ready to be shown for sale, agents contact buyers and arrange a convenient time for them to see the property. If the property is vacant, the broker usually retains the key. To adjust to the schedules of potential buyers, agents frequently show properties in the late afternoon or evening and on weekends. Because a representative of the broker's firm is usually on the premises in each house, weekend showings are a good way to put part-time or beginning agents to work.

An agent may have to meet several times with a prospective buyer to discuss and view available properties. When the buyer decides on a property, the agent must bring the buyer and seller together at terms agreeable to both. In many cases, different brokers will represent the seller and buyer. Agents may have to present several counteroffers to reach a compromise suitable to both parties.

Once the contract is signed by both the buyer and the seller, the agent must see to it that all terms of the contract are carried out before the closing date. For example, if the seller has agreed to repairs or a home inspection, the agent must make sure it is carried out or the sale cannot be completed.

Brokers often provide buyers with information on loans to finance their purchase. They also arrange for title searches and title insurance. A broker's knowledge, resourcefulness, and creativity in arranging financing that is favorable to the buyer can mean the difference between success and failure in closing a sale. In some cases, agents assume the responsibilities of closing the sale, but the closing process is increasingly handled by lawyers or loan officers.

Commercial or agricultural real estate agents operate in much the same fashion. Their clients usually have specific and prioritized needs. For example, a trucking firm might require their property to be located near major highways. These real estate specialists often conduct extensive searches to meet clients' specifications. They usually make fewer but larger sales, resulting in higher commissions.

In addition to selling real estate, some brokers rent and manage properties for a fee. Some brokers combine other types of work, such as selling insurance or practicing law, with their real estate businesses.

REQUIREMENTS
High School
There are no standard educational requirements for the real estate field. However, high school courses in English, business, and math would help to prepare you for communicating with clients and handling sales.

Postsecondary Training
An increasing percentage of real estate agents and brokers have some college education. As property transactions have become more complex, many employers favor applicants with more education. Courses in psychology, economics, sociology, marketing, finance, business administration, and law are helpful. Many colleges also offer specific courses or even degrees in real estate. More than 1,000 colleges, universities, and community colleges offer coursework in real estate.

Certification or Licensing
Every state (and the District of Columbia) requires that real estate agents and brokers be licensed. For the general license, most states

require agents to be at least 18 years old, have between 30 and 90 hours of classroom training, and pass a written examination on real estate fundamentals and relevant state laws. Prospective brokers must pass a more extensive examination and complete between 60 and 90 hours of classroom training. Additionally, many states require brokers to have prior experience selling property or a formal degree in real estate.

State licenses are usually renewed annually without examination, but many states require agents to fulfill continuing education requirements in real estate. Agents who move to another state must qualify under the licensing laws of that state. To supplement minimum state requirements, many agents take courses in real estate principles, laws, financing, appraisal, and property development and management.

Other Requirements
Successful brokers and agents must be willing to study the changing trends of the industry to keep their skills updated. Residential real estate agents must keep up with the latest trends in mortgage financing, construction, and community development. They must have a thorough knowledge of the housing market in their assigned communities so they can identify which neighborhoods will best fit their clients' needs and budgets, and they must be familiar with local zoning and tax laws. Agents and brokers must also be good negotiators to act as go-betweens between buyers and sellers.

In most cases, educational experience is less important than the right personality. Brokers want agents who possess a pleasant personality, exude honesty, and maintain a neat appearance. Agents must work with many different types of people and inspire their trust and confidence. They need to express themselves well and show enthusiasm to motivate customers. They should also be well organized and detail oriented, and have a good memory for names, faces, and business details.

EXPLORING
Contact local real estate brokers and agents for useful information on the field and to talk one-on-one with an employee about his or her job. You can also obtain information on licensing requirements from local real estate boards or from the real estate departments of each state. Securing part-time and summer employment in a real estate office will provide you with practical experience.

EMPLOYERS

There are approximately 564,000 real estate agents and brokers currently employed in the United States. Many work part time, supplementing their income with additional jobs in law, finance, or other fields.

Agents work in small offices, larger organizations, or for themselves. (Approximately 61 percent of real estate agents and brokers are self-employed.) Opportunities exist at all levels, from large real estate firms specializing in commercial real estate to smaller, local offices that sell residential properties. Much of agents' work is independent; over time, they can develop their own client bases and set their own schedules.

STARTING OUT

The typical entry position in this field is as an agent working for a broker with an established office. Another opportunity may be through inside sales, such as with a construction firm building new housing developments. Prospective agents usually apply directly to local real estate firms or are referred through public and private employment services. Brokers looking to hire agents may run newspaper advertisements. Starting out, prospective agents often contact firms in their own communities, where their knowledge of area neighborhoods can work to their advantage.

The beginning agent must choose between the advantages of joining a small or a large organization. In a small office, the newcomer will train informally under an experienced agent. Their duties will be broad and varied but possibly menial. However, this is a good chance to learn all the basics of the business, including gaining familiarity with the computers used to locate properties or sources of financing. In larger firms, the new agent often proceeds through a more standardized training process and specializes in one aspect of the real estate field, such as commercial real estate, mortgage financing, or property management.

ADVANCEMENT

While many successful agents develop professionally by expanding the quality and quantity of their services, others seek advancement by entering management or by specializing in residential or commercial real estate. An agent may enter management by becoming the head of a division of a large real estate firm. Other agents purchase an established real estate business, join one as a partner, or set up their own offices. Self-employed agents must meet state requirements and obtain a broker's license.

Agents who wish to specialize have a number of available options. They may develop a property management business. In return for approximately 5 percent of the gross receipts, *property managers* operate apartment houses or multiple-tenant business properties for their owners. Property managers are in charge of renting (including advertising, tenant relations, and collecting rents), building maintenance (heating, lighting, cleaning, and decorating), and accounting (financial recording and filing tax returns).

Agents can also become *appraisers*, estimating the current market value of land and buildings, or *real estate counselors*, advising clients on the suitability of available property. Experienced brokers can also join the real estate departments of major corporations or large government agencies.

EARNINGS

Compensation in the real estate field is based largely upon commission. Agents usually split commissions with the brokers who employ them, in return for providing the office space, advertising support, sales supervision, and the use of the broker's good name. When two or more agents are involved in a transaction (for example, one agent listing the property for sale and another selling it), the commission is usually divided between the two on the basis of an established formula. Agents can earn more if they both list and sell the property.

According to the U.S. Department of Labor, median annual earnings of salaried real estate agents, including commission, were $40,600 in 2007. Salaries ranged from less than $20,930 to more than $106,790.

Median annual earnings of salaried real estate brokers, including commission, were $58,860 in 2007, and the middle 50 percent of salaries for brokers ranged from less than $37,500 to more than $100,570 a year.

Agents and brokers may supplement their incomes by appraising property, placing mortgages with private lenders, or selling insurance. Since earnings are irregular and economic conditions unpredictable, agents and brokers should maintain sufficient cash reserves for slack periods.

Real estate agents and brokers who work for a company usually receive benefits such as vacation days, sick leave, health and life insurance, and a savings and pension program. Those who are self-employed must provide their own benefits.

WORK ENVIRONMENT

One glance at the property advertisements in any newspaper will offer a picture of the high degree of competition found within the field of real estate. In addition to full-time workers, the existence of many part-time agents increases competition.

Beginning agents must accept the frustration inherent in the early months in the business. Earnings are often irregular before a new agent has built a client base and developed the skills needed to land sales.

After agents become established, many work over 40 hours a week, including evenings and weekends to best cater to their clients' needs. Despite this, agents work on their own schedules and are free to take a day off when they choose. Some do much of their work out of their own homes. However, successful agents will spend little time in an office; they are busy showing properties to potential buyers or meeting with sellers to set up a listing.

Real estate positions are found in every part of the country but are concentrated in large urban areas and in smaller, rapidly growing communities. Regardless of the size of the community in which they work, good agents should know its economic life, the personal preferences of its citizens, and the demand for real estate.

OUTLOOK

According to the *Occupational Outlook Handbook,* employment of agents and brokers is expected to grow about as fast as the average for all occupations through 2016. Turnover within the field is high; new job opportunities surface as agents retire or transfer to other types of work.

The country's expanding population also creates additional demand for real estate services. A trend toward mobility, usually among Americans in their prime working years, indicates a continued need for real estate professionals. In addition, a higher percentage of affluence among this working group indicates that more Americans will be able to own their own homes.

An increase in agents' use of technology, such as computers, faxes, and databases, has greatly improved productivity. Real estate Web sites now allow agents and customers to view multiple property listings without leaving the office. However, the use of this technology may eliminate marginal jobs, such as part-time workers, who may not be able invest in this technology and compete with full-time agents. Job growth is potentially limited by the fact that many potential customers are conducting their own searches for property using the Internet.

The field of real estate is easily affected by changes in the economy. Periods of prosperity bring a lot of business. Conversely, a downturn leads to a lower number of real estate transactions, resulting in fewer sales and commissions for agents and brokers.

FOR MORE INFORMATION

For information on licensing, contact
Association of Real Estate License Law Officials
8361 South Sangre De Cristo Road, Suite 250
Littleton, CO 80127-4272
Tel: 303-979-6190
Email: mailbox@arello.org
http://www.arello.org

For information on state and local associations, professional designations, real estate courses, and publications, contact
National Association of Realtors
430 North Michigan Avenue
Chicago, IL 60611-4011
Tel: 800-874-6500
http://www.realtor.org

For information on commercial real estate, contact
Society of Industrial and Office Realtors
1201 New York Avenue, NW, Suite 350
Washington, DC 20005-6126
Tel: 202-449-8200
Email: admin@sior.com
http://www.sior.com

Retail Sales Managers

QUICK FACTS

School Subjects
Business
Mathematics

Personal Skills
Helping/teaching
Leadership/management

Work Environment
Primarily indoors
Primarily one location

Minimum Education Level
High school diploma

Salary Range
$21,760 to $34,470 to $60,550+

Certification or Licensing
Voluntary

Outlook
More slowly than the average

DOT
185

GOE
10.01.01

NOC
0621, 6211

O*NET-SOC
41-1011.00

OVERVIEW

Retail sales managers are responsible for the profitable operation of retail trade establishments. They oversee the selling of food, clothing, furniture, sporting goods, novelties, and many other items. Their duties include hiring, training, and supervising other employees, maintaining the physical facilities, managing inventory, monitoring expenditures and receipts, and maintaining good public relations. Retail sales managers hold about 2.2 million jobs in the United States.

HISTORY

In the United States, small, family owned stores have been around for centuries. The first large chain stores began to operate in the late 19th century when the Great Atlantic and Pacific Tea Company opened its first grocery store in 1859. That was followed in 1879 when the first F. W. Woolworth variety store opened. One of the aims of early chain stores was to provide staples for the pioneers of the newly settled West. Because chain store corporations were able to buy goods in large quantities and store them in warehouses, they were able to undersell private merchants.

The number of retail stores, especially supermarkets, began to grow rapidly during the 1930s. Stores often were owned and operated by chain corporations, which were able to benefit from bulk buying and more sophisticated storage practices. Cheaper transportation also contributed to the growth of retail stores because goods could be shipped and sold more economically.

Unlike the early family owned stores, giant retail outlets employed large numbers of people, requiring various levels of management to

A sales manager at a camping store gives a pep talk to his employees. (Mitch Wojnarowicz, The Amsterdam Recorder, The Image Works)

oversee the business. Retail managers were hired to oversee particular areas within department stores, for example, but higher-level managers also were needed to make more general decisions about a company's goals and policies. Today, retailing is the second largest industry in the United States, employing more than 24 million people.

THE JOB

Retail sales managers are responsible for every phase of a store's operation. They often are one of the first employees to arrive in the morning and the last to leave at night. Their duties include hiring, training, and supervising other employees, maintaining the physical facilities, managing inventory, monitoring expenditures and receipts, and maintaining good public relations.

Perhaps the most important responsibility of retail sales managers is hiring and training qualified employees. Managers then assign duties to employees, monitor their progress, promote employees, and increase salaries when appropriate. When an employee's performance is not satisfactory, a manager must find a way to improve the performance or, if necessary, fire him or her.

Managers should be good at working with all different kinds of people. Differences of opinion and personality clashes among employees are inevitable, however, and the manager must be able to restore good feelings among the staff. Managers often have to deal with upset customers, and must attempt to restore goodwill toward the store when customers are dissatisfied.

Retail sales managers keep accurate and up-to-date records of store inventory. When new merchandise arrives, the manager ensures items are recorded, priced, and displayed or shelved. They must know when stock is getting low and order new items in a timely manner.

Some managers are responsible for merchandise promotions and advertising. The manager may confer with an advertising agency representative to determine appropriate advertising methods for the store. The manager also may decide what products to put on sale for advertising purposes.

The duties of store managers vary according to the type of merchandise sold, the size of the store, and the number of employees. In small, owner-operated stores, managers often are involved in accounting, data processing, marketing, research, sales, and shipping. In large retail corporations, however, managers may be involved in only one or two activities.

REQUIREMENTS

High School

You will need at least a high school education in order to become a retail sales manager. Helpful courses include business, mathematics, marketing, and economics. English and speech classes are also important. These courses will teach you to communicate effectively with all types of people, including employees and customers.

Postsecondary Training

Most retail stores prefer management applicants with a college degree, and many hire only college graduates. Liberal arts, social sciences, and business are the most common degrees held by retail managers.

To prepare for a career as a retail store sales manager, take courses in accounting, business, marketing, English, advertising, and computer science. If you are unable to attend college as a full-time student, consider getting a job in a store to gain experience and attend college part time. All managers, regardless of their education, must have good marketing, analytical, communication, and people skills.

Many large retail stores and national chains have established formal training programs, including classroom instruction, for their new employees. The training period may last a week or as long as one year. Training for a department store manager, for example, may include working as a salesperson in several departments in order to learn about the store's operations.

Certification or Licensing
The National Retail Federation offers the voluntary national professional certification in retail management designation to managers who successfully pass an assessment and meet other requirements. Contact the federation for more information.

Other Requirements
To be a successful retail sales manager, you should have good communication skills, enjoy working with and supervising people, and be willing to put in very long hours. Diplomacy often is necessary when creating schedules for workers and in disciplinary matters. There is a great deal of responsibility in retail management and such positions often are stressful. A calm disposition and ability to handle stress will serve you well.

EXPLORING
If you are interested in becoming a retail sales manager, you may be able to find part-time, weekend, or summer jobs in a clothing

Most Popular Consumer Spending Holidays/Events, 2007

1. Winter Holidays:	$470.4 billion
2. Back to School/College:	$51.4 billion
3. Valentine's Day:	$17 billion
4. Mother's Day:	$15.8 billion
5. Easter:	$14.4 billion
6. Father's Day:	$9.6 billion
7. Super Bowl:	$9.5 billion
8. Halloween:	$5.77 billion
9. St. Patrick's Day:	$3.6 billion

Source: National Retail Federation

store, supermarket, or other retail trade establishment. You can gain valuable work experience through such jobs and will have the opportunity to observe the retail industry to determine whether you are interested in pursuing a career in it. It also is useful to read periodicals that publish articles on the retail field, such as *Stores* (http://www.stores.org), published by the National Retail Federation.

EMPLOYERS

There are about 2.2 million retail managers in the United States, and about 37 percent are self-employed (many are store owners). Nearly every type of retail business requires management, though small businesses may be run by their owners. Wherever retail sales are made there is an opportunity for a management position, though most people have to begin in a much lower job. The food industry employs more workers than nearly any other, and retail food businesses always need managers, though smaller businesses may not pay very well. In general, the larger the business and the bigger the city, the more a retail manager can earn. Most other retail managers work in grocery and department stores, motor vehicle dealerships, and clothing and accessory stores.

STARTING OUT

Many new college graduates are able to find managerial positions through their schools' career services office. Some of the large retail chains recruit on college campuses.

Not all store managers, however, are college graduates. Many store managers are promoted to their positions from jobs of less responsibility within their organization. Some may work in the retail industry for more than a dozen years before being promoted. Those with more education often receive promotions faster.

Regardless of educational background, people who are interested in the retail industry should consider working in a retail store at least part time or during the summer. Although there may not be an opening when the application is made, there often is a high turnover of employees in retail management, and vacancies occur frequently.

ADVANCEMENT

Advancement opportunities in retailing vary according to the size of the store, where the store is located, and the type of merchandise sold. Advancement also depends on the individual's work experience and educational background.

A store manager who works for a large retail chain, for example, may be given responsibility for a number of stores in a given area or region or transferred to a larger store in another city. Willingness to relocate to a new city may increase an employee's promotional opportunities.

Some managers decide to open their own stores after they have acquired enough experience in the retail industry. After working as a retail manager for a large chain of clothing stores, for example, a person may decide to open a small boutique.

Sometimes becoming a retail sales manager involves a series of promotions. A person who works in a supermarket, for example, may advance from clerk, checker, or bagger to a regular assignment in one of several departments in the store. After a period of time, he or she may become an assistant manager and eventually, a manager.

EARNINGS

Salaries depend on the size of the store, the responsibilities of the job, and the number of customers served. According to the U.S. Department of Labor, median annual earnings of supervisors of retail sales workers, including commission, were $34,470 in 2007. Salaries ranged from less than $21,760 to more than $60,550 per year. Mean annual earnings of grocery store managers were $36,850 in 2007, and managers of clothing stores earned $36,460. Those who managed other general merchandise stores earned $31,380, and those who managed building supply stores ranked among the highest paid at $41,430. Managers who oversee an entire region for a retail chain can earn more than $100,000.

In addition to a salary, some stores offer their managers special bonuses, or commissions, which are typically connected to the store's performance. Many stores also offer employee discounts on store merchandise.

WORK ENVIRONMENT

Most retail stores are pleasant places to work, and managers often are given comfortable offices. Many, however, work long hours. Managers often work six days a week and as many as 60 hours a week, especially during busy times of the year such as the Christmas season. Because holiday seasons are peak shopping periods, it is extremely rare that managers can take holidays off or schedule vacations around a holiday, even if the store is not open on that day.

Although managers usually can get away from the store during slow times, they must often be present if the store is open at night. It is important that the manager be available to handle the store's daily receipts, which usually are put in a safe or taken to a bank's night depository at the close of the business day.

OUTLOOK

Employment of retail sales managers is expected to grow more slowly than the average for all occupations through 2016, according to the U.S. Department of Labor. Although retailers have reduced their management staff to cut costs and make operations more efficient, there still are good opportunities in retailing. Internet stores and e-commerce ventures will present many new opportunities for retail managers, for example. However, competition for all jobs will probably continue to increase, and computerized systems for inventory control may reduce the need for some managers. Applicants with the best educational backgrounds and work experience will have the best chances of finding jobs. There will always be a need for retail sales managers, however, as long as retail stores exist. Retail sales manager positions are rarely affected by corporate restructuring at retail headquarters; this has a greater impact on home office staff.

FOR MORE INFORMATION

For information on certification and materials on educational programs in the retail industry, contact
National Retail Federation
325 Seventh Street, NW, Suite 1100
Washington, DC 20004-2818
Tel: 800-673-4692
http://www.nrf.com

For information on jobs in retail, contact
Retail Industry Leaders Association
1700 North Moore Street, Suite 2250
Arlington, VA 22209-1933
Tel: 703-841-2300
http://www.retail-leaders.org

Retail Sales Workers

OVERVIEW

Retail sales workers assist customers with purchases by identifying their needs, showing or demonstrating merchandise, receiving payment, recording sales, and wrapping their purchases or arranging for their delivery. They are sometimes called *sales clerks, retail clerks*, or *salespeople*. There are approximately 4.5 million retail salespersons employed in the United States.

HISTORY

The industrial revolution and its techniques of mass production encouraged the development of specialized retail establishments. The first retail outlets in the United States were trading posts and general stores. At trading posts, goods obtained from Native Americans were exchanged for items imported from Europe or manufactured in the eastern United States. Trading posts had to be located on the fringes of settlements and relocated to follow the westward movement of the frontier. As villages and towns grew, what had been trading posts frequently developed into general stores. General stores sold food staples, farm necessities, and clothing. They often served as the local post office and became the social and economic centers of their communities. They were sometimes known as dry goods stores.

A number of changes occurred in the retail field during the second half of the 19th century. The growth of specialized retail stores (such as hardware, feed, grocery, and drugstores) reflected the growing sophistication of available products and customer tastes. The first grocery chain store, which started in New York City in 1859, led to

QUICK FACTS

School Subjects
English
Mathematics
Speech

Personal Skills
Communication/ideas
Helping/teaching

Work Environment
Primarily indoors
Primarily one location

Minimum Education Level
High school diploma

Salary Range
$14,780 to $20,150 to $39,190+

Certification or Licensing
Voluntary

Outlook
About as fast as the average

DOT
290

GOE
10.03.01

NOC
6421

O*NET-SOC
41-2031.00

a new concept in retailing. Later, merchants such as Marshall Field developed huge department stores, so named because of their large number of separate departments. Their variety of merchandise, ability to advertise their products, and low selling prices contributed to the rapid growth and success of these stores. Retail sales workers staffed the departments, and they became the stores' primary representatives to the public.

The 20th century witnessed the birth of supermarkets and suburban shopping centers, the emergence of discount houses, and the expansion of credit buying. Today, retailing is the second largest industry in the United States. Grocery stores and chains have the highest annual sales in the retail field—followed, in order of size, by automobile dealers, department stores, restaurants and cafeterias, lumber and building suppliers, drug and proprietary stores, furniture stores, variety stores, liquor stores, hardware stores, and jewelry stores. All of these retailers hire sales workers.

THE JOB

Salespeople work in more than a hundred different types of retail establishments in a variety of roles. Some, for example, work in small specialty shops where, in addition to waiting on customers, they might check inventory, order stock from sales representatives (or by telephone or mail), place newspaper display advertisements, prepare window displays, and rearrange merchandise for sale.

Other salespeople may work in specific departments, such as the furniture department, of a large department store. The employees in a department work in shifts to provide service to customers six or seven days a week. To improve their sales effectiveness and knowledge of merchandise, they attend regular staff meetings. Advertising, window decorating, sales promotion, buying, and market research specialists support the work of retail salespeople.

Whatever they are selling, the primary responsibility of retail sales workers is to interest customers in the merchandise. This might be done by describing the product's features, demonstrating its use, or showing various models and colors. Some retail sales workers must have specialized knowledge, particularly those who sell such expensive, complicated products as stereos, appliances, and personal computers.

In addition to selling, most retail sales workers make out sales checks; receive cash, checks, and charge payments; bag or package purchases; and give change and receipts. Depending on the hours they work, retail sales workers might have to open or close the cash register. This might include counting the money in the cash register; separating charge slips, coupons, and exchange vouchers; and

A department store cashier checks out a customer. *(Matt York, AP Photo)*

making deposits at the cash office. The sales records they keep are normally used in inventory control. Sales workers are usually held responsible for the contents of their registers, and repeated shortages are cause for dismissal in many organizations.

Sales workers must be aware of any promotions the store is sponsoring and know the store's policies and procedures, especially on returns and exchanges. Also, they often must recognize possible security risks and know how to handle such situations.

Consumers often form their impressions of a store by its sales force. To stay ahead in the fiercely competitive retail industry, employers are increasingly stressing the importance of providing courteous and efficient service. When a customer wants an item that is not on the sales floor, for example, the sales worker might be expected to check the stockroom and, if necessary, place a special order or call another store to locate the item.

REQUIREMENTS

High School

Employers generally prefer to hire high school graduates for most sales positions. Such subjects as English, speech, and mathematics provide a good background for these jobs. Many high schools and two-year colleges have special programs that include courses in merchandising, principles of retailing, and retail selling.

Postsecondary Training

In retail sales, as in other fields, the level of opportunity tends to coincide with the level of a person's education. In many stores, college graduates enter immediately into on-the-job training programs to prepare them for management assignments. Successful and experienced workers who do not have a degree might also qualify for these programs. Useful college courses include economics, business administration, and marketing. Many colleges offer majors in retailing. Executives in many companies express a strong preference for liberal arts graduates, especially those with some business courses or a master's degree in business administration.

Certification and Licensing

The National Retail Federation offers the following voluntary designations to sales workers who successfully pass an assessment and meet other requirements: national professional certification in sales, national professional certification in customer service, and basics of retail credential. Contact the federation for more information.

Other Requirements

The retail sales worker must be in good health. Many selling positions require standing most of the day. The sales worker must have stamina to face the grueling pace of busy times, such as weekends and the Christmas season, while at the same time remaining pleasant and effective. Personal appearance is important. Salespeople should be neat and well groomed and have an outgoing personality.

A pleasant speaking voice, natural friendliness, tact, and patience are all helpful personal characteristics. The sales worker must be able to converse easily with strangers of all ages. In addition to interpersonal skills, sales workers must be equally good with figures. They should be able to add and subtract accurately and quickly and operate cash registers and other types of business machines.

Most states have established minimum standards that govern retail employment. Some states set a minimum age of 14, require at least a high school diploma, or prohibit more than eight hours of work a day or 48 hours in any six days. These requirements are often relaxed during the Christmas season.

EXPLORING

Because of its seasonal nature, retailing offers numerous opportunities for temporary or part-time sales experience. Most stores add extra personnel for the Christmas season. Vacation areas may hire sales employees, usually high school or college students, on a seasonal basis. Fewer sales positions are available in metropolitan areas during the summer, as this is frequently the slowest time of the year.

Many high schools and junior colleges have developed "distributive education" programs that combine courses in retailing with part-time work in the field. The distributive education student may receive academic credit for this work experience in addition to regular wages. Store owners cooperating in these programs often hire students as full-time personnel upon completion of the program.

EMPLOYERS

About 4.5 million people are employed as sales workers in retail stores of all types and sizes. There are many different types of retail establishments, ranging from small specialty shops that appeal to collectors to large retailers that sell everything from eyeglasses to DVD players. Department stores, building material and garden equipment stores, clothing and accessories stores, other general merchandise stores, and motor vehicle and parts dealers employ the largest number of retail salespersons. Retail sales workers can have just one or two coworkers or well over 100, depending on the size of the establishment.

STARTING OUT

If they have openings, retail stores usually hire beginning salespeople who come in and fill out an application. Major department stores maintain extensive personnel departments, while in smaller stores the manager might do the hiring. Occasionally, sales applicants are given an aptitude test.

Young people might be hired immediately for sales positions. Often, however, they begin by working in the stockroom as clerks, helping to set up merchandise displays, or assisting in the receiving or shipping departments. After a while they might be moved up to a sales assignment.

Training varies with the type and size of the store. In large stores, the beginner might benefit from formal training courses that cover sales techniques, store policies, the mechanics of recording sales, and an overview of the entire store. Programs of this type are usually followed by on-the-job sales supervision. The beginner in a small store might receive personal instruction from the manager or a senior sales worker, followed by supervised sales experience.

College graduates and people with successful sales experience often enter executive training programs (sometimes referred to as flying squads because they move rapidly through different parts of the store). As they rotate through various departments, the trainees are exposed to merchandising methods, stock and inventory control, advertising, buying, credit, and personnel. By spending time in each of these areas, trainees receive a broad retailing background designed to help them as they advance into the ranks of management.

ADVANCEMENT

Large stores have the most opportunities for promotion. Retailing, however, is a mobile field, and successful and experienced people can readily change employment. This is one of the few fields where, if the salesperson has the necessary initiative and ability, advancement to executive positions is possible regardless of education.

When first on the job, sales workers develop their career potential by specializing in a particular line of merchandise. They become authorities on a certain product line, such as sporting equipment, women's suits, or building materials. Many good sales workers prefer the role of the *senior sales worker* and remain at this level. Others might be asked to become supervisor of a section. Eventually they might develop into a *department manager, floor manager, division or branch manager,* or *general manager.*

People with sales experience often enter related areas, such as buying. Other retail store workers advance into support areas, such as personnel, accounting, public relations, and credit.

Young people with ability find that retailing offers the opportunity for unusually rapid advancement. One study revealed that half of all retail executives are under 35 years of age. It is not uncommon for a person under 35 to be in charge of a retail store or department with an annual sales volume of over $1,000,000. Conversely, a retail executive who makes bad merchandising judgments might quickly be out of a job.

EARNINGS

Most beginning sales workers start at the federal minimum wage, which increased to $7.25 an hour in 2009. Wages vary greatly, depending primarily on the type of store and the degree of skill required. Businesses might offer higher wages to attract and retain workers. Some sales workers make as much as $12 an hour or more.

Department stores or retail chains might pay more than smaller stores. Higher wages are paid for positions requiring a greater degree of skill. Many sales workers also receive a commission (often 4 to 8 percent) on their sales or are paid solely on commission. According to the U.S. Department of Labor, median hourly earnings of retail salespersons, including commission, were $9.69 in 2007. A yearly salary for full-time work therefore averages $20,150. Wages ranged from less than $7.11 ($14,780 a year) to more than $18.84 an hour ($39,190 a year). Sales workers earned the following mean hourly salaries by industry sector: new and used car dealerships, $21.52; building material and supplies dealers, $12.80; clothing stores, $9.88; and department stores, $9.65.

Salespeople in many retail stores are allowed a discount on their own purchases, ranging from 10 to 25 percent. This privilege is sometimes extended to the worker's family. Meals in the employee cafeterias maintained by large stores might be served at a price that is below cost. Many stores provide sick leave, medical and life insurance, and retirement benefits for full-time workers. Most stores give paid vacations.

WORK ENVIRONMENT

Retail sales workers generally work in clean, comfortable, well-lighted areas. Those with seniority have reasonably good job security. When business is slow, stores might curtail hiring and not fill vacancies that occur. Most stores, however, are able to weather mild recessions in business without having to release experienced sales workers. During periods of economic recession, competition among salespeople for job openings can become intense.

With nearly two million retail stores across the country, sales positions are found in every region. An experienced salesperson can find employment in almost any state. The vast majority of positions, however, are located in large cities or suburban areas.

The five-day, 40-hour workweek is the exception rather than the rule in retailing. Most salespeople can expect to work some evening and weekend hours, and longer than normal hours might be scheduled during Christmas and other peak periods. In addition, most retailers restrict the use of vacation time between Thanksgiving and early January. Most sales workers receive overtime pay during Christmas and other rush seasons. Part-time salespeople generally work at peak hours of business, supplementing the full-time staff. Because competition in the retailing business is keen, many retailers work under pressure. The sales worker might not be directly involved but will feel the pressures of the industry in subtle ways. The sales worker must be able to adjust to alternating periods of high activity and dull monotony. No two days—or even customers—are alike. Because some customers are hostile and rude, salespeople must learn to exercise tact and patience at all times.

OUTLOOK

About 4.5 million people are employed as sales workers in retail stores of all types and sizes. The employment of sales personnel should grow about as fast as the average for all occupations through 2016, according to the U.S. Department of Labor. Turnover among sales workers is much higher than average, which will create good employment opportunities in this large field. Many of the expected employment opportunities will stem from the need to replace workers. Other positions will result from existing stores' staffing for longer business hours or reducing the length of the average employee workweek. Employment opportunities are predicted to be the strongest at warehouse clubs and supercenters, according to the U.S. Department of Labor.

As drug, variety, grocery, and other stores have rapidly converted to self-service operations, they will need fewer sales workers. At the same time, many products, such as stereo components, cell phones, electrical appliances, computers, and sporting goods, do not lend themselves to self-service operations. These products require extremely skilled sales workers to assist customers and explain the benefits of various makes and models. On balance, as easy-to-sell goods will be increasingly marketed in self-service stores, the demand in the future will be strongest for sales workers who are knowledgeable about particular types of products.

During economic recessions, sales volume and the resulting demand for sales workers generally decline. Purchases of costly items, such as cars, appliances, and furniture, tend to be postponed during difficult economic times. In areas of high unemployment, sales of all types of goods might decline. Since turnover of sales workers is usually very high, however, employers often can cut payrolls simply by not replacing all those who leave.

There should continue to be good opportunities for temporary and part-time workers, especially during the holidays. Stores are particularly interested in people who, by returning year after year, develop good sales backgrounds.

FOR MORE INFORMATION

For information on certification and educational programs in the retail industry, contact
National Retail Federation
325 Seventh Street, NW, Suite 1100
Washington, DC 20004-2818
Tel: 800-673-4692
http://www.nrf.com

INTERVIEW

Tom Bagby works as a retail sales worker for a small chain of pharmacies. He discussed his career with the editors of Careers in Focus: Sales.

Q. Can you please describe a typical day in your life on the job?
A. My typical weekday shift starts at 4 P.M. after school and lasts four hours. I clock in and then meet briefly with my manager to talk about any issues that have come up during the day (new sales, problems with cash registers, new training protocols, etc.). Then I begin working the register—ringing up sales. I also answer customer questions and help them find products, put away new stock, do light cleaning (sweeping and dusting shelves), and straighten the products on the shelves (known as "facing"). On Saturdays, I start at 9 A.M. and usually work till 2 P.M.

I have different duties if I'm working as a delivery driver. In that case, I might work the cash register until the deliveries are ready to go out. At that time, someone takes over for me at the cash register, and I deliver pharmaceuticals and other goods (aspirin, vitamins, paper goods, etc.) to our customers. I travel anywhere from around the block (I usually walk these deliveries) to up to about five miles away to bring the deliveries to our customers. Once I'm done with the deliveries, I return to one of the stores and work the cash register or do other duties until more deliveries are ready to go out.

Q. What are the most important personal and professional qualities for retail sales workers?
A. You really need strong communication and people skills to be successful in this job. You will interact with people of all ages and from all backgrounds throughout your shift, including coworkers, managers, and customers. You also need to be honest, hard working, and able to follow directions.

Q. What activities would you suggest to high school students who are interested in this career?
A. This is one of the easiest fields to get experience in while still in high school. Get a job at your local drugstore, a store at the mall, or a local fast food restaurant.

Q. What are some of the pros and cons of your job?
A. No day is ever the same. I really like interacting with customers and enjoy the hustle and bustle of our stores. It's also nice to

develop relationships with customers. Some people have been coming into our stores for years, so gradually I get to learn about their lives and their families.

Cons include having to be on your feet for long stretches at a time, the low pay, and having to work set hours.

Q. What advice would you give to other young people who are interested in the field?

A. Working in retail sales is a great job for high school students, but you should probably avoid a sales job if you don't like working with people. Work in this field is an excellent starting point if you would like to pursue a career in sales—including working your way up to managerial positions.

Sales Managers

OVERVIEW

Sales managers direct a company's sales program by managing staff, working with dealers and distributors, setting prices for products and services, analyzing sales data, establishing sales goals, and implementing plans that improve sales performance. They may oversee an entire company, a geographical territory of a company's operations, or a specific department within a company. There are approximately 318,000 sales managers employed in the United States.

HISTORY

For as long as products and services have been sold, there has been a need for sales managers to manage staff, create sales strategies, oversee the distribution or delivery of goods and services, and establish training programs for sales workers. Sales managers are key players in businesses of all types and sizes.

THE JOB

Most companies that have a national or regional presence employ sales managers to manage the activity of their stores, the merchandise or services sold, and the performance of their sales staff. They may be in charge of multiple stores as determined by their territory. Some sales managers oversee territories that encompass a section of a large city, while others cover entire regions of the United States or abroad.

Sales managers oversee activities of each store's sales staff within their assigned territory. They implement training programs for employees to improve the work flow, interaction with customers, and familiarity with the company's products or services. Sales managers set

QUICK FACTS

School Subjects
Business
Mathematics

Personal Skills
Helping/teaching
Leadership/management

Work Environment
Primarily indoors
One location with some travel

Minimum Education Level
Bachelor's degree

Salary Range
$45,860 to $94,910 to $145,600+

Certification or Licensing
None available

Outlook
About as fast as the average

DOT
164

GOE
10.01.01

NOC
0611

O*NET-SOC
11-2022.00

sales goals for each salesperson, store managers, and the store itself. They monitor a store or stores' monthly or quarterly sales figures to ensure they meet set sales quotas. If not, they make recommendations to increase sales figures. These might include creating new sales presentations or special advertising programs or implementing employee retraining. Sales managers also work with each store manager to devise seasonal advertising campaigns and establish marketing budgets.

If their parent company offers franchising opportunities, sales managers are often responsible for interviewing and assessing potential owners. They explain company policies, procedures, and the principles behind its products or services. Sales managers may analyze potential market locations to determine if a new store would be viable. Once a new franchise is operational, sales managers visit often to inspect the store to ensure it is meeting company safety codes, procedures, and marketing plans.

Sales managers also oversee the quality and quantity of products sold or services rendered. For example, the regional sales manager of a national jewelry chain may inspect the loose diamonds or other gemstones that are purchased from wholesalers to determine if they meet the standards of the parent company. They may increase merchandise orders for each store to keep inventory levels sufficient during holidays or other times of the year when sales increase.

Sales managers may also be involved in product research and development. For example, district or regional managers of stores specializing in home goods may be instrumental in finding new furniture lines, kitchenware, or other accessories to carry in their stores. They often maintain contact with dealers and distributors to ensure imported goods arrive safely and in a timely manner, as well as meet governmental import regulations and procedures.

In addition to being familiar with their store's products, sales managers must also be knowledgeable about their company's work processes. For example, a district sales manager for the McDonald's Corporation must know the proper way to cook, prep, and package each food item on the company's menu.

Other duties of sales managers include monitoring the purchasing preferences of customers, writing reports, and representing the company at trade shows, conventions, and association meetings.

REQUIREMENTS

High School

If you are interested in a career as a sales manager, you should start preparing in high school by taking college preparatory classes. Because strong communication skills are important, take as many English classes as possible. Speech classes are another way to improve your communication skills. Courses in mathematics, accounting, statistics, business, marketing, advertising, economics, and computer science are also excellent choices to help you prepare for this career.

Postsecondary Training
Many sales managers have a bachelor's degree in business administration, with an emphasis on marketing or sales. Approximately 66 percent of sales managers between the ages of 25 and 44 years have a bachelor's degree or higher. Useful general college classes include those in psychology, sociology, business, and economics. Managers often have graduate and professional degrees.

Because managers coordinate the efforts of their whole departments, most have worked in lower-level sales jobs. Candidates for managerial positions who have extensive experience will have a competitive edge.

Other Requirements
There are a number of personal characteristics that you will need to succeed in this career—including good communication and interpersonal skills, strong organizational skills, and the ability to delegate work to members of your staff. The ability to think on your feet and work well under pressure is also critical.

Other traits considered important for sales managers are intelligence, decisiveness, intuition, creativity, strategic vision, honesty, loyalty, and a sense of responsibility.

EXPLORING

You can explore this career by developing your managerial skills in general. Whether you're involved in drama, sports, school publications, or a part-time job, there are managerial duties associated with any organized activity. These can involve planning, scheduling, managing other workers or volunteers, fund-raising, or budgeting.

EMPLOYERS

There are approximately 318,000 sales managers in the United States. Most work in finance, insurance, manufacturing, retail trade, and the wholesale trade industries.

STARTING OUT

You will first need experience in lower-level sales jobs before advancing to a managerial position. To break into a sales position, contact your college career services office for assistance. In addition, many firms advertise job listings in newspapers and Internet job boards.

Your first few jobs in sales should give you experience in working with clients, studying the market, and following up on client service. This work will give you a good sense of the rhythm of the job and the type of work required.

ADVANCEMENT

Most management and top executive positions are filled by experienced lower-level workers who have displayed valuable skills, such as leadership, self-confidence, creativity, motivation, decisiveness, and flexibility. In smaller firms, advancement to a management position may come slowly, while promotions may occur more quickly in larger firms.

Advancement may be accelerated by participating in advanced training programs sponsored by industry and trade associations or by enrolling in continued education programs at local universities. These programs are sometimes paid for by the firm. Managers committed to improving their knowledge of the field and of related disciplines—especially computer information systems—will have the best opportunities for advancement.

EARNINGS

The median annual earnings for sales managers were $94,910 in 2007, according to the U.S. Department of Labor (USDL). The lowest paid 10 percent earned $45,860 or less, while the highest paid 25 percent earned $145,600 or more.

Salary levels vary substantially, depending upon the level of responsibility, length of service, and type, size, and location of the company. Top-level managers in large companies can earn much more than their counterparts in small companies. Also, salaries in large metropolitan areas, such as New York City, are higher than those offered in smaller cities.

Benefit and compensation packages for managers are usually excellent, and may even include such things as bonuses, stock awards, and company-paid insurance premiums.

WORK ENVIRONMENT

Sales managers are provided with comfortable offices near the departments they direct. Higher-level managers may have spacious, lavish offices and may enjoy such privileges as executive dining rooms, company cars, country club memberships, and liberal expense accounts.

Managers often work long hours under intense pressure to meet sales goals. Workweeks consisting of 55 to 60 hours at the office are not uncommon—in fact, some higher-level managers spend up to 80 hours working each week. These long hours limit time available for family and leisure activities.

Sales departments—especially those at large companies—are usually highly charged with energy and are both physically and psychologically exciting places to work. Managers work with others as a team in a creative environment where a lot of ideas are exchanged among colleagues.

OUTLOOK

Employment of sales managers is expected to grow about as fast as the average for all occupations through 2016, according to the U.S. Department of Labor. The outlook for sales managers is closely tied to the overall economy. When the economy is good, business expands both in terms of the company's output and the number of people it employs, which creates a need for more managers. In economic downturns, firms often lay off employees and cut back on production, which lessens the need for managers. Opportunities are expected to be strongest in scientific, professional, and related services companies, and much weaker in manufacturing industries.

Many job openings will be the result of managers being promoted to better positions, retiring, or leaving their positions to start their own businesses. Even so, the compensation and prestige of these positions make them highly sought-after, and competition to fill openings will be intense. College graduates with experience, a high level of creativity, and strong communication skills should have the best job opportunities.

FOR MORE INFORMATION

For news about management trends and resources on career information and finding a job, contact
   American Management Association
   Tel: 877-566-9441
   http://www.amanet.org

For information on the practice, study, and teaching of marketing, contact
   American Marketing Association
   311 South Wacker Drive, Suite 5800
   Chicago, IL 60606-6629

Tel: 800-262-1150
http://www.marketingpower.com

For a brochure on a career in management, contact
National Management Association
2210 Arbor Boulevard
Dayton, OH 45439-1506
Tel: 937-294-0421
Email: nma@nma1.org
http://nma1.org

For information on jobs in retail, contact
Retail Industry Leaders Association
1700 North Moore Street, Suite 2250
Arlington, VA 22209-1933
Tel: 703-841-2300
http://www.retail-leaders.org

Sales Representatives

OVERVIEW

Sales representatives, also called *sales reps*, sell the products and services of manufacturers and wholesalers. They look for potential customers or clients such as retail stores, other manufacturers or wholesalers, government agencies, hospitals, and other institutions; explain or demonstrate their products to these clients; and attempt to make a sale. The job may include follow-up calls and visits to ensure the customer is satisfied.

Sales representatives work under a variety of titles. Those employed by manufacturers are typically called *manufacturers' sales workers* or *manufacturers' representatives*. Those who work for wholesalers are sometimes called *wholesale trade sales workers* or *wholesale sales representatives*. A *manufacturers' agent* is a self-employed salesperson who agrees to represent the products of various companies. A *door-to-door sales worker* usually represents just one company and sells products directly to consumers, typically in their homes. Approximately 2 million people work as manufacturers' and wholesale sales representatives in the United States.

HISTORY

Sales representatives for manufacturers and wholesalers have long played an important role in the U.S. economy. By representing products and seeking out potential customers, they have helped in the efficient distribution of large amounts of merchandise.

QUICK FACTS

School Subjects
Business
Mathematics
Speech

Personal Skills
Communication/ideas
Helping/teaching

Work Environment
Indoors and outdoors
Primarily multiple locations

Minimum Education Level
High school diploma

Salary Range
$26,490 to $59,510 to $128,550+

Certification or Licensing
None available

Outlook
About as fast as the average

DOT
250, 251, 252, 253, 254, 259, 260, 261, 262, 269, 270, 271, 272, 273, 274, 275, 276, 277, 279, 291

GOE
10.01.01, 10.02.01, 10.03.01, 10.04.01

NOC
6221, 6411, 6421, 6433

O*NET-SOC
41-4011.00, 41-4011.01, 41-4011.02, 41-4011.03, 41-4011.04, 41-4011.05, 41-4011.06, 41-4012.00, 41-9031.00, 41-9091.00

The earliest wholesalers were probably the ship "chandlers," or suppliers, of colonial New England, who assembled in large quantities the food and equipment required by merchant ships and military vessels. Ship owners found that a centralized supply source enabled them to equip their vessels quickly.

Various developments in the 19th century made wholesalers more prominent. Factories were becoming larger, thus allowing for huge amounts of merchandise to be manufactured or assembled in a single location. New forms of transportation, especially the railroad, made it more practical for manufacturers to sell their products over great distances. Although some manufacturers would sell their goods directly to retail outlets and elsewhere, many found it easier and more profitable to let wholesalers do this job. Retail stores, moreover, liked working with wholesalers, who were able to sell them a wide range of merchandise from different manufacturers and from different areas of the country and the world.

The sales representatives hired by manufacturers and wholesalers were typically given a specific territory in which to sell their goods. Armed with illustrated product catalogs, special promotional deals, and financial support for advertising, they traveled to prospective customers and tried to explain the important qualities of their products. Competition between sales representatives sometimes was fierce, leading some to be less than scrupulous. Product claims were exaggerated, and retail stores were sometimes supplied with shoddy merchandise. Eventually more fact-based sales pitches were emphasized by manufacturers and wholesalers, who in the long run benefited from having responsible, honest, well-informed representatives. Products also began to be backed by written guarantees of quality.

Meanwhile, some manufacturers were employing door-to-door sales workers to sell their products directly to consumers. Direct selling in the United States goes back to the famous "Yankee Peddler" who, during colonial times, traveled by wagon, on horseback, and sometimes on foot, bringing to isolated settlers many products that were not easily available otherwise. A forerunner of the modern door-to-door sales worker, peddlers also tried to anticipate the settlers' needs and wants. They frequently represented new or unknown products with the hope of creating a demand for them.

Changes in the 20th century, once again including improvements in transportation, brought still more possibilities for sales representatives. Automobiles allowed representatives to travel to many more communities and to carry more product samples and descriptive catalogs. Trucks provided a new means of transporting merchandise. The growth of commercial aviation further expanded the opportunities for salespeople. Sales representatives would eventually be able to travel to customers in New York, Atlanta, Los Angeles, and Minneapolis, for example, all during a single week.

Today, the food products industry is one of the largest employers of sales representatives. Other important fields include printing, publishing, fabricated metal products, chemicals and dyes, electrical and other machinery, and transportation equipment. Among the many establishments helped by sales representatives are retail outlets, which need a constant supply of clothing, housewares, and other consumer goods, and hospitals, which purchase specialized surgical instruments, drugs, rubber gloves, and thousands of other products from representatives.

THE JOB

Manufacturers' representatives and wholesale sales representatives sell goods to retail stores, other manufacturers and wholesalers, government agencies, and various institutions. They usually do so within a specific geographical area. Some representatives concentrate on just a few products. An electrical appliance salesperson, for example, may sell 10 to 30 items ranging from food freezers and air-conditioners to waffle irons and portable heaters. Representatives of drug wholesalers, however, may sell as many as 50,000 items.

The duties of sales representatives usually include locating and contacting potential new clients, keeping a regular correspondence with existing customers, determining their clients' needs, and informing them of pertinent products and prices. They also travel to meet with clients, show them samples or catalogs, take orders, arrange for delivery, and possibly provide installation. A sales representative also must handle customer complaints, keep up to date on new products, and prepare reports. Many salespeople attend trade conferences, where they learn about products and make sales contacts.

Finding new customers is one of sales representatives' most important tasks. Sales representatives often follow leads suggested by other clients, from advertisements in trade journals, and from participants in trade shows and conferences. They may make "cold calls" to potential clients. Sales representatives frequently meet with and entertain prospective clients during evenings and weekends.

Representatives who sell highly technical machinery or complex office equipment often are referred to as *sales engineers* or *industrial sales workers*. Because their products tend to be more specialized and their clients' needs more complex, the sales process for these workers tends to be longer and more involved. Before recommending a product, they may, for example, carefully analyze a customer's production processes, distribution methods, or office procedures.

They usually prepare extensive sales presentations that include information on how their products will improve the quality and efficiency of the customer's operations.

Some sales engineers, often with the help of their company's research and development department, adapt products to a customer's specialized needs. They may provide the customer with instructions on how to use the new equipment or work with installation experts who provide this service. Some companies maintain a sales assistance staff to train customers and provide specific information. This permits sales representatives to devote a greater percentage of their time to direct sales contact.

Other sales workers, called *detail people*, do not engage in direct selling activities but strive instead to create a better general market for their companies' products. A detail person for a drug company, for example, may call on physicians and hospitals to inform them of new products and distribute samples.

The particular products sold by the sales representative directly affect the nature of the work. Salespeople who represent sporting goods manufacturers may spend most of their time driving from town to town calling on retail stores that carry sporting equipment. They may visit with coaches and athletic directors of high schools and colleges. A representative in this line may be a former athlete or coach who knows intimately the concerns of his or her customers.

Food manufacturers and wholesalers employ large numbers of sales representatives. Because these salespeople usually know the grocery stores and major chains that carry their products, their main focus is to ensure the maximum sales volume. Representatives negotiate with retail merchants to obtain the most advantageous store and shelf position for displaying their products. They encourage the store or chain to advertise their products, sometimes by offering to pay part of the advertising costs or by reducing the selling price to the merchant so that a special sale price can be offered to customers. Representatives check to make sure that shelf items are neatly arranged and that the store has sufficient stock of their products.

Sales transactions can involve huge amounts of merchandise, sometimes worth millions of dollars. For example, in a single transaction, a washing-machine manufacturer, construction company, or automobile manufacturer may purchase all the steel products it needs for an extended period of time. Salespeople in this field may do much of their business by telephone because the product they sell is standardized and, to the usual customer, requires no particular description or demonstration.

Direct, or door-to-door, selling has been an effective way of marketing various products, such as appliances and housewares, cookware, china, tableware and linens, foods, drugs, cosmetics and toiletries, costume jewelry, clothing, and greeting cards. Like other sales representatives, door-to-door sales workers find prospective buyers, explain and demonstrate their products, and take orders. Door-to-door selling has waned in popularity, and Internet-based selling has taken over much of the door-to-door market.

Several different arrangements are common between companies and their door-to-door sales workers. Under the direct company plan, for example, a sales representative is authorized to take orders for a product, and the company pays the representative a commission for each completed order. Such workers may be employees of the company and may receive a salary in addition to a commission, or they may be independent contractors. They usually are very well trained. Sales workers who sell magazine subscriptions may be hired, trained, and supervised by a *subscription crew leader*, who assigns representatives to specific areas, reviews the orders they take, and compiles sales records.

Under the exhibit plan a salesperson sets up an exhibit booth at a place where large numbers of people are expected to pass, such as a state fair, trade show, or product exposition. Customers approach the booth and schedule appointments with the salespersons for later demonstrations at home.

The dealer plan allows a salesperson to function as the proprietor of a small business. The salesperson, or dealer, purchases the product wholesale from the company and then resells it to consumers at the retail price, mainly through door-to-door sales.

Under various group plans, a customer is contacted by a salesperson and given the opportunity to sponsor a sales event. In the party plan, for example, the sales representative arranges to demonstrate products at the home of a customer, who then invites a group of friends for the party. The customer who hosts the party receives free or discounted merchandise in return for the use of the home and for assembling other potential customers for the salesperson.

Finally, the COD plan allows representatives to sell products on a cash-on-delivery (COD) basis. In this method, the salesperson makes a sale, perhaps collecting an advance deposit, and sends the order to the company. The company, in turn, ships the merchandise directly to the customer, who in this case makes payment to the delivery person, or to the salesperson. The product is then delivered to the customer and the balance collected.

Whatever the sales plan, door-to-door sales workers have some advantages over their counterparts in retail stores. Direct sellers, for example, do not have to wait for the customer to come to them; they go out and find the buyers for their products. The direct seller often carries only one product or a limited line of products and thus is much more familiar with the features and benefits of the merchandise. In general, direct sellers get the chance to demonstrate their products where they will most likely be used—in the home.

There are drawbacks to this type of selling. Many customers grow impatient or hostile when salespeople come to their house unannounced and uninvited. It may take several visits to persuade someone to buy the product. In a brief visit, the direct seller must win the confidence of the customer, develop the customer's interest in a product or service, and close the sale.

REQUIREMENTS

High School
A high school diploma is required for most sales positions, although an increasing number of salespeople are graduates of two- or four-year colleges. In high school, take classes such as business, mathematics, psychology, speech, and economics that will teach you to deal with customers and financial transactions.

Postsecondary Training
Some areas of sales work require specialized college work. Those in engineering sales, for example, usually have a college degree in a relevant engineering field. Other fields that demand specific college degrees include chemical sales (chemistry or chemical engineering), office systems (accounting or business administration), and pharmaceuticals and drugs (biology, chemistry, or pharmacy). Those in less technical sales positions usually benefit from course work in English, speech, psychology, marketing, public relations, economics, advertising, finance, accounting, and business law. Approximately 53 percent of sales representatives had an associate's degree or higher in 2006, according to the U.S. Department of Labor.

Certification or Licensing
The Manufacturers' Representatives Educational Research Foundation offers several certification designations for sales representatives who are employed by manufacturers. Contact the foundation for more information.

Other Requirements
To be a successful sales representative, you should enjoy working with people. You should also be self-confident and enthusiastic, and self-disciplined. You must be able to handle rejection since only a small number of your sales contacts will result in a sale.

EXPLORING

If you are interested in becoming a sales representative, try to get part-time or summer work in a retail store. Working as a telemarketer also is useful. Some high schools and junior colleges offer programs that combine classroom study with work experience in sales.

Various opportunities exist to gain experience in direct selling. You can take part in sales drives for school or community groups, for instance.

Occasionally manufacturers hire college students for summer assignments. These temporary positions provide an opportunity for the employer and employee to appraise each other. A high percentage of students hired for these specialized summer programs become career employees after graduation. Some wholesale warehouses also offer temporary or summer positions.

EMPLOYERS

In the United States, 2 million people work as manufacturers' and wholesale sales representatives. Nearly 60 percent of these salespeople work in wholesale, many as sellers of machinery. Many others work in mining and manufacturing. Food, drugs, electrical goods, hardware, and clothing are among the most common products sold by sales representatives.

STARTING OUT

Manufacturing and wholesale firms looking for sales representatives sometimes list job openings with high school and college career services offices as well as with public and private employment agencies. In many areas, professional sales associations refer people to suitable openings. Contacting companies directly also is recommended. A list of manufacturers and wholesalers can be found in telephone books and industry directories, which are available at public libraries.

Although some high school graduates are hired for manufacturers' or wholesale sales jobs, many join a company in a nonselling position, such as office, stock, or shipping clerk. This experience allows an employee to learn about the company and its products. From there, he or she eventually may be promoted to a sales position.

Most new representatives complete a training period before receiving a sales assignment. In some cases new salespeople rotate through several departments of an organization to gain a broad exposure to the company's products. Large companies often use formal training programs lasting two years or more, while small organizations frequently rely on supervised sales experience.

Direct selling usually is an easy field to enter. Direct sale companies advertise for available positions in newspapers, in sales workers' specialty magazines, and on television and radio. Many people enter direct selling through contacts they have had with other door-to-door sales workers. Most firms have district or area representatives who interview applicants and arrange the necessary training. Part-time positions in direct selling are common.

ADVANCEMENT

New representatives usually spend their early years improving their sales ability, developing their product knowledge, and finding new clients. As sales workers gain experience they may be shifted to increasingly large territories or more difficult types of customers. In some organizations, experienced sales workers narrow their focus. For example, an office equipment sales representative may work solely on government contracts.

Advancement to management positions, such as *regional* or *district manager*, also is possible. Some representatives, however, choose to remain in basic sales. Because of commissions, they often earn more money than their managers do, and many enjoy being in the field and working directly with their customers.

A small number of representatives decide to become *manufacturers' agents*, or self-employed salespeople who handle products for various organizations. Agents perform many of the same functions as sales representatives but usually on a more modest scale.

Door-to-door sales workers also have advancement possibilities. Some are promoted to supervisory roles and recruit, train, and manage new members of the sales force. Others become *area, branch,* or *district managers*. Many managers of direct selling firms began as door-to-door sales workers.

EARNINGS

Many beginning sales representatives are paid a salary while receiving their training. After assuming direct responsibility for a sales territory, they may receive only a commission (a fixed percentage of each dollar sold). Also common is a modified commission plan (a lower rate of commission on sales plus a low base salary). Some companies provide bonuses to successful representatives.

Because manufacturers' and wholesale sales representatives typically work on commission, salaries vary widely. Some made as little as $26,490 a year in 2007, according to the U.S. Department of Labor (USDL). The most successful representatives earned more than $128,550. However, the median annual salaries for sales representatives working with technical and scientific products were $68,270, and $50,750, including commissions, for those working in other aspects of wholesale and manufacturing. Most sales representatives make between $35,000 and $71,000 a year.

Earnings can be affected by changes in the economy or industry cycles, and great fluctuations in salary from year to year or month to month are common. Employees who travel usually are reimbursed for transportation, hotels, meals, and client entertainment expenses. Door-to-door sales workers usually earn a straight commission on their sales, ranging from 10 to 40 percent of an item's suggested retail price.

Sales engineers earned salaries that ranged from less than $48,290 to $131,780 or more in 2007, according to the USDL.

Sales representatives typically receive vacation days, medical and life insurance, and retirement benefits. However, manufacturers' agents and some door-to-door sales workers do not receive benefits.

WORK ENVIRONMENT

Salespeople generally work long and irregular hours. Those with large territories may spend all day calling and meeting customers in one city and much of the night traveling to the place where they will make the next day's calls and visits. Sales workers with a small territory may do little overnight travel but, like most sales workers, may spend many evenings preparing reports, writing up orders, and entertaining customers. Several times a year, sales workers may travel to company meetings and participate in trade conventions and conferences. Irregular working hours, travel, and the competitive demands of the job can be disruptive to ordinary family life.

Sales work is physically demanding. Representatives often spend most of the day on their feet. Many carry heavy sample cases or catalogs. Occasionally, sales workers assist a customer in arranging a display of the company's products or moving stock items. Many door-to-door sellers work in their own community or nearby areas, although some cover more extensive and distant territories. They often are outdoors in all kinds of weather. Direct sellers must treat customers, even those who are rude or impatient, with tact and courtesy.

OUTLOOK

Employment for manufacturers' and wholesale sales representatives is expected to grow about as fast as the average for all careers through 2016, according to the U.S. Department of Labor (USDL). Because of continued economic growth and an increasing number of new products on the market, more sales representatives will be needed to explain, demonstrate, and sell these products to customers. The USDL notes that job opportunities will be better for wholesale and manufacturing sales representatives who specialize in technical and scientific products, but competition for in-house sales positions with wholesalers will be stiff, and jobs will go to applicants with the most experience and technical knowledge.

Independent sales workers, who are paid exclusively on a commission basis, should have strong employment opportunities.

Future opportunities will vary greatly depending upon the specific product and industry. For example, as giant food chains replace independent grocers, fewer salespeople will be needed to sell groceries to individual stores. By contrast, greater opportunities will probably exist in the air-conditioning field, and advances in consumer electronics and computer technology also may provide many new opportunities.

FOR MORE INFORMATION

For a list of marketing programs and detailed career information, contact

Direct Marketing Association
1120 Avenue of the Americas
New York, NY 10036-6700
Tel: 212-768-7277
http://www.the-dma.org

For referrals to industry trade associations, contact

Manufacturers' Agents National Association
One Spectrum Pointe, Suite 150
Lake Forest, CA 92630-2282
Tel: 877-626-2776
Email: MANA@MANAonline.org
http://www.manaonline.org

Services Sales Representatives

OVERVIEW

Services sales representatives sell a variety of services, from furniture upholstery and graphic arts to pest control and telephone communications systems. In general, they try to find potential clients, describe or demonstrate the services to them, answer any questions they may have, and attempt to make sales. Services sales representatives usually telephone their customers or travel to their homes or places of business. Some, however, work out of an office and meet clients who come to them.

HISTORY

For many centuries, people who performed services for a living did not have to advertise. Blacksmiths, weavers, printers, and other workers relied on word of mouth from satisfied customers to get new business. As cities grew, however, competition among tradespeople increased. As a result, businesses selling services began to hire sales agents who could contact potential clients and interest those clients in their services.

The invention of the telephone and improvements in travel have greatly expanded the territory that services sales representatives can cover. Companies that offer very specialized services can approach clients all over the country or the world. The direct selling of services has developed along the same lines as the direct selling of products; the sales representative has become the key to

QUICK FACTS

School Subjects
Business
Mathematics

Personal Skills
Communication/ideas
Helping/teaching

Work Environment
Primarily indoors
Primarily multiple locations

Minimum Education Level
High school diploma

Salary Range
$24,650 to $48,550 to $101,260+

Certification or Licensing
Voluntary

Outlook
Faster than the average

DOT
251

GOE
10.02.01, 10.02.02

NOC
6411, 6421

O*NET-SOC
41-3099.00, 41-4011.00, 41-4011.01, 41-4011.02, 41-4011.03, 41-4011.04, 41-4011.05, 41-4011.06, 41-4012.00

the successful interaction between those who need services and those who provide them.

THE JOB

Although specific job responsibilities depend on the type of service being sold, all services sales representatives have a variety of duties in common. For example, most contact prospective clients, try to determine the clients' needs, and describe or demonstrate the pertinent services. It is vital that sales representatives understand and be able to discuss the services provided by their company. For example, a services sales representative who works for a shipping company must be familiar with shipping rates, import and export regulations, industry standards, and a host of other factors involving packaging and handling.

The sales procedure usually begins with developing lists of prospective clients. A sales representative may be able to form a list from telephone and business directories, by asking existing customers and other business associates for leads, or by receiving inquiries from potential customers. The representative can then call the potential clients and either begin the sales pitch over the phone or set up a meeting. Sales pitches typically are made in person, as they often require the use of literature or a demonstration of the service. Sales representatives also try to analyze their clients' specific needs and answer any questions they may have.

Keeping in constant touch with customers and potential customers is another important component of the job. If he or she fails to make a sale to a potential customer, for example, the services sales representative may follow up with more visits, letters, and phone calls. Periodic contact with customers can encourage the continued use of the services and increases the likelihood that a customer will recommend the services to friends or business acquaintances.

Job responsibilities vary with the size of the company. Representatives working for large companies generally have more specialized responsibilities and are assigned to specific territorial boundaries. Those who work for small companies may have public relations and administrative tasks in addition to their sales responsibilities.

There are many specialized jobs within the services sales field. These include *sales-service promoters,* who create goodwill for companies by attending appropriate conventions and advising other sales representatives on ways to increase sales of a particular service. Sales representatives sell warehouse space and services to manufacturers and others who need it.

Data-processing services sales representatives sell various complex services, such as inventory control and payroll processing, to companies using computers in their business operations. *Travelers' checks sales representatives* visit banks, consumer groups, and travel agencies to explain the benefits of travelers' checks. *Business services sales agents* sell business services, such as linen supply and pest control services, usually within a specified territory.

Financial-report service sales agents sell such services as credit and insurance investigation reports to stores and other business establishments. *Communications consultants* discuss communications needs with residential and commercial customers and suggest services that would help clients meet those needs. *Telephone services sales representatives* visit commercial customers to review their telephone systems, analyze their communications needs and, if necessary, recommend additional telecommunication services.

Public utilities sales representatives visit commercial and residential customers to promote economical use of gas, electricity, or telephone service. They quote rates for changes in service and installation charges.

Advertising sales representatives sell advertising space or broadcast time to advertising firms or to other companies that maintain their own advertising departments. *Hotel services sales representatives* contact business, government, and social groups to solicit conference and convention business for their hotels. *Group sales representatives* work for sports teams or other entertainment organizations and promote group ticket sales or season ticket sales. They also may arrange for group seating and special activities on the day of the event. *Sales promotion representatives* visit retail outlets and encourage the use of display items, such as posters, that can increase retail sales.

Education courses sales representatives recruit students for technical or commercial training schools. They inform prospective applicants of enrollment requirements and tuition fees. *Psychological test and industrial relations sales agents* sell programs of psychological, intelligence, and aptitude tests to businesses and schools. They aid in integrating the programs into the school or business operation and help in the administration, scoring, and interpretation of the tests.

Other services sales representatives sell pest control services, franchises, herbicide services, shipping services, graphic art services, signs and displays, printing, audiovisual program production, electroplating, elevators and escalators, and television cable service.

REQUIREMENTS

High School
For most sales positions, a college degree is required, though some companies of nontechnical services hire high school graduates. For

example, a company that sells laundry services may accept applications from high school graduates. High school students should take college preparatory courses, including English, speech, mathematics, and history.

Postsecondary Training
The more complex a service, the greater the likelihood of the need for a higher level of education. For example, a company that markets advertising services would likely seek a sales representative with an undergraduate degree in advertising or a master's degree in business administration.

College programs vary depending on your particular area of interest but may include course work in psychology, marketing, public relations, finance, and business law.

Certification or Licensing
Certification is becoming more common for services sales representatives. Sales and Marketing Executives International (SME) offers the following certifications: certified marketing executive, certified sales executive, and SME certified professional salesperson. Contact SME for more information on certification requirements.

Other Requirements
It is important for salespeople to work well with other people. You should be sincere, tactful, cheerful, optimistic, and sociable with both acquaintances and strangers. You must be able to make a good initial impression and maintain it while working repeatedly with the same customers.

Many services sales representatives work without direct supervision and create their own schedules. For this type of work, you must be efficient and well organized and have sufficient self-motivation to continue to pursue potential customers even after a long day or a series of setbacks.

EXPLORING

Because many services require that salespeople have specialized knowledge, untrained workers have few opportunities to explore the field directly. Students, however, can measure their abilities and interest in sales work by finding a part-time sales job in a store. In addition, some school work-study programs offer opportunities with local businesses for part-time, practical on-the-job training. It may also be helpful to read periodicals, such as *Selling Power* (http://www.sellingpower.com), that publish articles on the sales field.

EMPLOYERS

About half of all services sales representatives work for firms providing business services, including computer and data processing, advertising, personnel, equipment rental, mailing, printing, and stenographic services.

STARTING OUT

Because maturity and the ability to work independently are so important, many employers prefer to hire people who have achieved success in other jobs, either in sales or in a related field. Small companies in particular are reluctant to hire applicants without previous sales experience. In contrast, extremely large companies sometimes prefer applicants who are recent college graduates.

For those entering the job market just out of college, school career services offices may be helpful in supplying job leads. In addition, those interested in securing an entry-level position can contact appropriate companies directly. Jobs may also be located through help wanted advertisements.

Most new sales representatives must complete a training period before receiving their first sales assignment. Large companies may use formal training classes that last several months, while smaller organizations may emphasize supervised sales experience.

Selling highly technical services, such as communications or computer systems, usually involves more complex and lengthy sales training. In these situations, sales representatives usually work as part of a team and receive technical assistance from support personnel. For example, those who sell telecommunications equipment may work with a communications consultant.

ADVANCEMENT

The primary form of advancement for services sales representatives is an increase in the number and size of accounts they handle and, possibly, an increase in their sales territory. Some experienced representatives with leadership ability become *branch office managers* and supervise other sales representatives. A few representatives advance to top management positions or become partners in their companies. Some go into business for themselves.

It is not unusual for someone to begin as a sales representative and then enter a related position with a company. For example, a successful sales representative may become a purchasing agent or a marketing executive.

EARNINGS

Earnings for services sales representatives depend on a number of variables, including sales skills, the quality of the services, geographic location, the number of potential customers and their need for the services, and the health of the economy. A beginning services sales representative can expect to earn between $20,000 and $25,000 a year. According to the U.S. Department of Labor, median annual earnings of all sales representatives, services, were $48,550, including commission, in 2007. Salaries ranged from less than $24,650 to more than $101,260.

Representatives who work for large companies can earn salaries of $100,000 or higher annually. Extremely successful sales representatives (especially those who sell technical services) can earn more than $128,000. Experienced sales workers often earn more than their branch managers. It is important to realize, however, that the amount of sales in almost every industry is directly affected by the overall economy. Because sales can go up and down frequently, earnings can fluctuate widely.

Sales representatives work on different types of compensation plans. Some get a straight salary; others are paid commissions based on the total volume of sales. Most sales representatives are paid a combination of salary, commission, and bonuses. Bonuses may be based on the increase in number of new clients brought to the company or an increase in overall sales. Bonuses may amount to several thousand dollars at some companies.

WORK ENVIRONMENT

Services sales representatives work long and irregular hours. Sales workers with large territories frequently spend all day calling on customers in one city and then travel to another city to make calls the next day. Many sales representatives spend at least several nights a month away from home. Those sales workers with limited territories may have less overnight travel, but, like all sales workers, they may have to spend many evenings preparing reports, writing up orders, and entertaining customers and potential customers. Some representatives who sell primarily by phone spend the majority of their time in the office.

Although most services sales representatives work long hours and make appointments to fit the convenience of customers, they usually have a considerable amount of flexibility. They can set their own schedules as long as they meet their company's goals.

Sales work is physically demanding. Sales representatives may spend most of the day on their feet. Many travel constantly from one place to another. Sales workers also face competition from other representatives and the possibility that their customers may switch their business to another organization. This, coupled with the uncertainty of sales during tough economic times, can add greatly to the stress of the job.

OUTLOOK

Employment opportunities for services sales representatives are expected to grow faster than the average for all occupations through 2016, depending on the service involved. The Internet has had a significant impact in all sales fields. Consumers are now able to shop wider markets and compare prices. A Web site can perform many of the sales functions that once required people—describing services, demonstrating them, and offering price quotes. Computer and data-processing services sales should continue to be strong, and faster-than-average growth is expected in the number of advertising sales representatives.

As with other sales occupations, the high turnover among services sales representatives will lead to many new job openings each year, especially for those who sell non-technical services. Those with the most education, training, and sales experience will have the best job opportunities.

FOR MORE INFORMATION

For career and education information, contact
Manufacturers' Representatives Educational Research Foundation
8329 Cole Street
Arvada, CO 80005-5834
Tel: 303-463-1801
http://www.mrerf.org

For information on careers and certification, contact
Sales and Marketing Executives International
PO Box 1390
Sumas, WA 98295-1390
Tel: 312-893-0751
http://www.smei.org

Wireless Sales Workers

QUICK FACTS

School Subjects
Business
Speech

Personal Skills
Communication/ideas

Work Environment
Primarily indoors
One location with some travel

Minimum Education Level
High school diploma

Salary Range
$35,000 to $68,000 to $110,000

Certification or Licensing
None available

Outlook
Faster than the average

DOT
N/A

GOE
N/A

NOC
N/A

O*NET-SOC
41-3099.99

OVERVIEW

Wireless sales workers, also known as *wireless* or *cellular sales representatives*, work for wireless telecommunications service providers to sell products and services to individuals and businesses. The products and services they sell include cellular phones, phone service, pagers, paging service, and various wireless service package options. Inside sales workers work on-site at their employers' sales offices, helping customers who come in to inquire about wireless service. Outside sales workers travel to call on various potential customers at their offices.

HISTORY

Although you may think of cellular phones as being a product of late 20th century technology, they actually have their beginnings all the way back in the late 1800s. In 1895, an Italian electrical engineer and inventor named Guglielmo Marconi figured out how to transmit signals from one place to another using electromagnetic waves, creating the first radio. One of Marconi's first major successes came in 1896, when he was able to send signals over a distance of more than a mile. Marconi continued to improve and refine his invention. In 1897, he transmitted signals from shore to a ship at sea 18 miles away, and in 1901, he sent signals a distance of 200 miles. By 1905, many ships were regularly using Marconi's radio to communicate with the shore.

Radio evolved rapidly. By the mid-1920s, more than 1,400 radio stations were broadcasting programming all across America, and by the end of the 1940s, that number had grown to 2,020. Immediately following World War II, radio saw a period of especially rapid development and improvement. Sophisticated transmitting and receiving equipment played a key role in the exploration of space, and in 1969, astronauts on the Apollo mission used a very high-frequency radio communication system to transmit their voices from the Moon back to Earth for the first time.

Cellular radio, which is essentially today's cellular phone service, was first tested in the United States in the 1970s. This system, a miniature version of large radio networks, was named cellular because its broadcast area is divided into units called cells. Each cell was equipped with its own radio transmitter, with a range of about one to 2.5 miles. As a mobile radiophone moved through this network of cells, its calls were switched from one cell to another by a computerized system. It was possible to make calls only within the area covered by the network of cells, however; once the radiophone was outside the cellular area, the connection was lost. First tested in Chicago and the Washington, D.C., area, this cellular system was soon duplicated in other towns, both large and small, throughout the United States. As more and more of the United States became covered with these networks of cells, it became possible to use cellular phones in more places and use of these phones became increasingly widespread.

In order to use a cellular phone, one had to have two things: the phone itself and a subscription to a cellular service. Cellular service providers, much like traditional phone companies, signed up users for phone service to be billed on a monthly basis. Often, as part of the sign-up agreement, the new customer received a free or inexpensive cellular phone. As the availability of cellular service has expanded geographically, the number of people signing up for this service has increased dramatically. According to CTIA-The Wireless Association, in 2008 approximately 263 million Americans were wireless service subscribers. Cellular, or wireless, sales workers in communities across the United States have been the liaison between the cellular providers and the cellular users. They have been the workers selling the service, explaining its workings, and signing up these new users.

THE JOB

Wireless sales workers sell communications systems, equipment, and services to both businesses and individuals. The products they sell may be divided up into "hard" products—such as pagers or cellular phones—and "soft" products, such as cellular phone service, paging service, voice mail, or phone service options. Most wireless sales workers work for a cellular service provider, trying to persuade prospective buyers to sign up for that provider's phone service. In areas that are covered by two or more cellular providers, the salesperson may have to convince customers to use his or her provider instead of the competition. In other cases, it is merely a matter of convincing the customer that he or she needs cellular service, explaining what the service provides, and doing the paperwork to begin a contract.

There are two categories of wireless sales workers. Outside sales workers visit prospective clients at their offices. These workers may make appointments in advance, or they may drop in unannounced and ask for a few minutes of the prospective customer's time. This practice is called cold calling. Outside sales workers often call on customers only within a specific geographic territory that may be defined by their employers. Members of the second category, inside sales workers, work in a cellular provider's offices, frequently in a customer showroom. These workers greet and help customers who come into the office to buy or inquire about wireless services. Brian Quigley is the inside sales manager for a major cellular service provider in Bloomington, Indiana. Before becoming the manager, he worked as a sales representative for four years.

There are several aspects of a wireless sales representative's job. The first is generating new customers. Sales workers develop lists of possible customers in many different ways. They may ask for referrals from existing customers, call on new businesses or individuals as they move into their assigned territory, or compile names and numbers from business directories or phone books. They may also attend business trade shows or expositions, or join networking groups where they can make contact with people who might be interested in signing up for their service. Once sales workers have their list of possible contacts, they may send out letters or sales brochures, often following up with a phone call and a request for an appointment.

The second aspect of the job is perhaps the most important. This involves talking with prospective customers about the company's services and products and helping them choose the ones that they will be happy with. In order to do this, the sales worker must have a thorough knowledge of all the company's offerings and be able to explain how these offerings can meet the customer's needs. "We spend a lot of time each day taking sales calls from people or working with walk-ins," Quigley says. "And dealing with people who are considering buying wireless is not a quick process. On the average, you spend between 15 and 30 minutes with one customer, answering all of his or her questions." Answering these questions may involve demonstrating the features of different phones or pagers, going over the pricing structures of various service plans, or explaining how the wireless service works and what its geographic limitations are. The sales worker must try to overcome any objections the customer might have about the products or services and convince him or her to make the purchase. If the salesperson fails to "close the deal" on the first visit, he or she might follow up with more visits, phone calls, or letters.

A wireless sales worker's job usually involves a certain amount of paperwork. When a salesperson makes a sale, he or she may input the customer's billing and credit information into a computer in order to generate a contract, explain the contract to the customer, and ask him or her to sign it. He or she may also do the paperwork necessary to activate the new customer's phone or pager. Sales workers may also maintain records on all their customers, usually in a computer database.

Many sales workers maintain contact with their customers even after making a sale. The salesperson may make a follow-up call to ensure that the customer's service or product is working properly and that he or she is satisfied. The salesperson may also check back periodically to see if the customer is interested in purchasing "upgrades"—new or improved services or products. The sales reps in Quigley's location also help existing customers who have questions about their equipment, service, or billing statement. "You'd be surprised how much of my job is servicing existing customers," he says. "I'll bet I spend 80 percent of my time on customer retention."

Because wireless technology changes so rapidly, learning about new products and services is an important part of a wireless sales worker's job. He or she may frequently attend seminars or training programs to keep current on the latest in wireless products, in order to be able to explain them to potential customers. Quigley says that his company holds quarterly sales rallies, where wireless equipment manufacturers come to explain and demonstrate their new products. "A lot of the stuff you just have to learn on your own, too," he says. "Because things change so rapidly, you often can't wait until the next sales rally to find out about a piece of equipment. You just have to crack open the manual and read up on it."

REQUIREMENTS

High School

The minimum educational level needed to become a wireless sales worker is a high school diploma. To prepare for a career in wireless sales, you should choose high school classes that will help you understand and communicate with people. Courses in speech, English, and psychology are all good options for this. You might also want to take classes that help you understand basic business principles, such

172 Careers in Focus: Sales

A sales worker discusses wireless plan options with a customer. *(Paul Sakuma, AP Photo)*

as business and math courses. Finally, it may be helpful to take some fundamental computer classes in order to become familiar with keyboarding and using some basic software applications. Like virtually all other offices, wireless offices are typically computerized—so you will probably need to be comfortable using a computer.

Postsecondary Training

Although there are no formal requirements, it is becoming more and more common for wireless sales workers to have a two- or four-year college degree. Brian Quigley began his career in wireless sales after obtaining a bachelor's degree in marketing, and he says that his company prefers to recruit college graduates. Many employers consider a bachelor's degree in marketing, business, or telecommunications to be especially beneficial. In addition, because wireless services are so heavily dependent on technology, some wireless sales workers enter the field with a technology-related degree.

Whether a new wireless sales worker has a college degree or not, there are likely to be aspects of the job and the company that he or she is not familiar with. Therefore, most wireless service companies provide training programs for their newly hired workers. These programs, which may last from three weeks to three months, cover such topics as cellular technologies, product lines, sales techniques, using the company's computer system, entering orders, and other company policies.

Other Requirements

Successful wireless sales workers have a combination of personal characteristics that allow them to do their jobs well. Perhaps the most important is the ability to connect and communicate with people; without this quality, it is virtually impossible to be an effective salesperson. Wireless salespersons should enjoy interacting with people, feel comfortable talking with people they do not know, and be able to communicate clearly and persuasively. "You also have to be a good listener, in addition to a good talker," Quigley says. "When someone is upset, you have to hear what they are saying and be able to appease them." The ability to work in a high-pressure, competitive environment is also an important characteristic. Many wireless sales workers earn the majority of their income from commissions or bonuses. In addition, most workers are expected to meet monthly or quarterly sales goals that are set by the company. Successful sales workers should be able to handle the stress of working to meet these goals. Self-confidence is another essential quality of good sales workers. Any sales job will involve a certain amount of rejection from customers who are not interested or not ready to buy. Salespersons must be secure and confident enough to avoid letting this rejection affect them on a personal level. According to Quigley, the willingness to learn and change is also highly important to success in this field. "This industry is always changing, sometimes so quickly that it's hard to keep up with it," he says. "You have to be prepared for the changes."

EXPLORING

You can find out what it is like to be a wireless sales worker by visiting the offices of a local cellular provider. By talking with the sales staff and perhaps observing them as they work, you should be able to get a feel for what the day-to-day job entails. One of the best ways to find out firsthand if you enjoy selling is to find a summer or after-school job in sales. To learn more about wireless technology and the products available, visit your local library and see what books and magazine articles are available—or do some online research on the Internet.

EMPLOYERS

Most of the major telecommunications companies throughout the United States offer wireless service in addition to their traditional phone service. For example, AT&T, Sprint Nextel, MCI Verizon, and U.S. Cellular all have wireless divisions—and, consequently, wireless sales staff. These providers are located all throughout the United States, in virtually every medium-sized and large community. You should be able to find a list of them by asking your local librarian for help or by doing a keyword search on "wireless service providers" on the Internet.

STARTING OUT

To find a job in wireless sales, you should first determine which wireless service providers operate in your area. Check directly with these providers to find out if they have any openings, or send them a resume and cover letter. If you are willing to relocate, you might contact the national headquarters of each of the large wireless companies mentioned earlier to find out what jobs are available nationwide. Many of these companies also have current job openings posted on their Web sites. You might also keep an eye on local or regional newspapers. Telecommunications companies, including wireless providers, frequently post job openings in the classified sections of these newspapers. If you have attended a college or university, check with your school's career services office to see if it has any contacts with wireless service providers.

Many wireless providers prefer to hire applicants with proven sales records. This may be especially true in cases where the applicant has only a high school diploma. If you find that you are having difficulty obtaining a position in wireless sales, you might consider first taking another sales job (perhaps in electronic or communications equipment) to gain experience. Once you have proven your abilities, you may have better luck being hired for a wireless sales position.

ADVANCEMENT

For most wireless salespersons, advancement comes in the form of increased income via commissions and bonuses. A proven sales worker might earn the title of *senior sales representative* or *senior account executive*. These workers may be given better territories or larger, more important accounts to handle. Some sales workers eventually move into managerial roles as they expand in their capabilities and knowledge of the company. A sales worker might move into the position of *sales manager,* for example. In this position, he or she would oversee other salespersons, either for the entire organization or for a specific geographic territory. Brian Quigley became the sales manager for his location after four years of working as a sales representative. The next step on the career ladder for him is *general manager of retail stores,* which would put him in charge of a specific geographic region. Another advancement possibility in larger companies is that of *trainer*. In the role of sales trainer, a sales worker would be responsible for developing, coordinating, and training new employees in sales techniques.

EARNINGS

For motivated and skilled salespersons, the pay for wireless sales can be quite good. Most companies offer their sales staff a small base salary and incentive pay in the form of commissions, bonuses, or both. In

Top U.S. Wireless Carriers By Market Share, 2007

AT&T:	27.1 percent
Verizon:	26.3 percent
Sprint Nextel:	23.6 percent
Other:	11.9 percent
T-Mobile:	11.1 percent

Source: Forrester Research

some cases, the incentive pay can increase the salesperson's base salary by up to 75 percent. Because most salespersons earn the majority of their income through incentive pay, the income level depends greatly upon individual performance.

According to the *U.S. News & World Report*'s "Best Jobs for the Future," the average beginning wireless sales worker might expect to earn around $35,000. A senior sales worker might earn around $68,000, and a top sales executive can make as much as $110,000. Wireless sales managers can expect to earn between $75,000 and $80,000.

Sales workers who are employed by most wireless companies receive a benefits package, which typically includes health insurance and paid vacation, sick days, and holidays. Outside sales workers may be provided with a company car and an expense account to pay for food, lodging, and travel expenses incurred while traveling on company business.

WORK ENVIRONMENT

Inside sales representatives typically work in comfortable, attractively decorated customer showrooms. They usually have desks either in the showroom or in a back office, where they can do their paperwork and perhaps meet with customers. While many sales reps work regular 40-hour weeks, Monday through Friday, it is not at all uncommon for these workers to work longer-than-average weeks. In addition, many wireless sales offices are open on weekends to accommodate customers who cannot come in during the week. Therefore, some sales workers spend weekend hours at the office.

Outside sales workers may spend much of their time traveling to meet on-site with various potential customers. Unless a salesperson's territory is very large, however, overnight travel is uncommon. When not traveling, outside sales workers may spend time in the office, setting up appointments with customers, keeping records, and completing paperwork. Both types of sales workers spend the majority of their time dealing with people. In addition to customer contact, these salespersons often work cooperatively with service technicians and customer service staff.

OUTLOOK

Job opportunities for wireless sales workers are expected to grow at a rate that is faster than the average. CTIA-The Wireless Association estimates that there are approximately 63,000 new wireless subscribers every day. The sales of pagers and paging services has also grown tremendously. Part of the reason for this growth is that technological advances are making wireless phones and pagers more effective and useful all the time. One of the most recent developments, digital communication technology, has increased wireless phone use by offering better quality and range (98 percent of all wireless subscribers are now digital). Wireless service is also being increasingly used to transmit data as well as voice. Examples of wireless data communication include such applications as texting, faxing, and Internet access. In addition, new technology, widespread use of wireless services, and more leverage for the consumer as a result of federal legislation (such as being able to change providers and keeping the same wireless phone number) have driven the prices of service down. This means that wireless services are now an option for many people who previously couldn't afford them. All of these factors combined should spur the need for a growing number of sales workers. The demand for jobs will also be enhanced by the high turnover in the sales field as a whole. Each year, many sales workers leave their jobs—in wireless and other industries—because they fail to make enough money or feel they are not well suited to the demanding career. New sales workers must then be hired to replace those who have left the field.

FOR MORE INFORMATION

For job postings, links to wireless industry recruiters, industry news, and training information, contact or visit the following Web site:
    CTIA-The Wireless Association
    1400 16th Street, NW, Suite 600
    Washington, DC 20036-2225
    Tel: 202-785-0081
    http://www.ctia.org

For the latest on the wireless industry and job information, contact
    Wireless Industry Association
    8665 West Flamingo, Suite 200
    Las Vegas, NV 89147-8621
    Tel: 800-624-6918
    Email: contact@wirelessindustry.com
    http://wirelessdealers.com

For a brochure on mobile phone etiquette and other information on the wireless industry in Canada, contact
Canadian Wireless Telecommunications Association
130 Albert Street, Suite 1110
Ottawa, ON K1P 5G4 Canada
Tel: 613-233-4888
Email: info@cwta.ca
http://www.cwta.ca

Index

Entries and page numbers in **bold** indicate major treatment of a topic.

A

AAF. *See* American Advertising Federation
"absolute" (bidding process) 21
Accenture 59, 60
account executives. *See* advertising account executives; financial services brokers
accredited auctioneer real estate 24
accredited purchasing practitioner 114
ACH Direct (Allen, TX) 104
ACNA. *See* Antiques and Collectibles National Association
advertising account executives 5–11
Advertising Age 8
Advertising Educational Foundation 10
Adweek 8
agents. *See* insurance agents and brokers; purchasing agents; real estate agents and brokers
AICPCU. *See* American Institute for Chartered Property and Casualty Underwriters
Amazon.com 95, 96, 99
American Advertising Federation (AAF) 11
American Association of Advertising Agencies 11
American Association of University Professors 46
American College 84, 89, 91
American Federation of Teachers 46
American Institute for Chartered Property and Casualty Underwriters (AICPCU) 84, 89–90
American International Automobile Dealers 38
American Management Association 149
American Marketing Association 11, 39, 46, 149–150
American Marketing Society. *See* American Marketing Association
American Purchasing Society 112, 114, 115, 118
Anderson Consulting. *See* Accenture
antiques and art dealers 12–19
Antiques and Collectibles National Association (ACNA) 12, 17, 18
Antiques Roadshow 16, 19

APICS-The Association for Operations Management 115, 118
appraisers 125. *See also* antiques and art dealers; real estate agents and brokers
architects 103. *See also* Internet transaction specialists
area managers 158. *See also* sales representatives
art dealers. *See* antiques and art dealers
Art Dealers Association of America 18
Association for Computing Machinery 64–65
Association for Operations Management 114
Association of Professional Insurance Women 90
Association of Real Estate License Law Officials 127
AT&T 174, 175
Auctioneer (periodical) 25
auctioneers 20–28
auction houses 16
auction technology specialists 24
automobile dealerships 30–31
automobile sales workers 29–38
Automotive Careers Today 38
Automotive Retailing Today 37
AutoNation 38

B

Babylonia, development of insurance 79
Bagby, Tom 143–144
Bartels, Robert 39
benefit auctioneer specialists 24
Best Buy 64, 99
"Big Three" automobile makers 29
branch managers 140, 148. *See also* retail sales workers; sales representatives
branch office managers 87, 165. *See also* insurance agents and brokers; service sales representatives
Brandweek 8
brokers. *See* commodities brokers; financial services brokers; insurance agents and brokers; real estate agents and brokers
business services sales representatives 163. *See also* service sales representatives
Butler, Ralph S. 39
buyers. *See* media buyers; purchasing agents

179

180 Careers in Focus: Sales

C

Canadian Wireless Telecommunications Association 178
CarMax 38
cash-on-delivery (COD) sales plan 155
casualty insurance. *See* property and casualty insurance
CBOE. *See* Chicago Board Options Exchange
cellular phones, development of 168–169
cellular sales representatives. *See* wireless sales workers
Center for Futures Education 55
CERT 111
"certificates of receipt" 47
certification and licensing
  antiques and art dealers 15
  auctioneers 23, 24
  automobile sales workers 34
  commodities brokers 51
  counter and rental clerks 68
  financial services brokers 74–75
  insurance agents and brokers 84–85
  Internet store managers and entrepreneurs 98
  Internet transaction specialists 106
  purchasing agents 114–115
  real estate agents and brokers 122–123
  retail sales managers 131
  sales representatives 156
  service sales representatives 164
certified estate specialist 24
certified insurance counselor 84
certified insurance service representative 84
certified marketing executive 164
certified professional in supply management 114
certified professional public buyer 114–115
certified professional purchasing manager 115
certified professional salesperson 164
certified public purchasing officer 114
certified purchasing professional 115
certified sales executive 164
certified supply chain professional 115
Chartered Financial Consultant. *See* ChFC
Chartered Life Underwriter. *See* CLU
chartered property casualty underwriter (CPCU) 84, 89
ChFC (Chartered Financial Consultant) 89
Chicago, IL 8, 9, 25
Chicago Board of Trade. *See* CME Group
Chicago Board Options Exchange (CBOE) 55
Chicago Mercantile Exchange. *See* CME Group
China, development of insurance 78
Christie's (auction house) 16, 20
Chrysler Corporation 29
Clio Awards 8
CLU (Chartered Life Underwriter) 89
CME Group 48, 50, 52, 56
Code of Fair Competition for the Motor Vehicle Retailing Trade 30
Code of Hammurabi 79
COD sales plan. *See* cash-on-delivery sales plan
"cold calls" 73, 153
collectibles market 12–13
Collectors.org 19
college professors, sales and marketing 39–46
commission (salary) 26
commodities brokers 47–57
commodity futures contracts 48
Commodity Futures Trading commission 56
communications consultants 163. *See also* service sales representatives
computer and electronics sales representatives 58–65
Computer Security Institute 111
ComputerWorld 109
Corrales, Ron 59–64
correspondence instructors 41. *See also* college professors, sales and marketing
counter and rental clerks 66–71
CPCU. *See* chartered property casualty underwriter
Crossroads magazine 64
CTIA-The Wireless Association 169, 176–177
cybercrime 104

D

data-processing services sales representatives 162–163. *See also* service sales representatives
dealer sales plan 155
dealerships. *See* automobile dealerships
DeBower, H. 39
department managers 140. *See also* retail sales workers
detail people 154. *See also* sales representatives

Dictionary of Occupational Titles (DOT) 2, 3
direct company sales plan 155
Direct Marketing Association 160
direct selling 154–156
discount brokers 48. *See also* commodities brokers
distance learning instructors 41. *See also* college professors, sales and marketing
district managers 158. *See also* sales representatives
division managers 140. *See also* retail sales workers
Dojima Rice Market 47
door-to-door sales workers 158. *See also* sales representatives
door-to-door selling. *See* direct selling
DOT. *See Dictionary of Occupational Titles*
dot-com businesses 110

E

eBay.com 99
e-commerce 101
Eddie Bauer (Internet store) 96
education courses sales representatives 163. *See also* service sales representatives
EFT. *See* electronic funds transfer
electronic funds transfer (EFT) 104–105
Electronics Representatives Association International 65
electronics sales representatives. *See* computer and electronics sales representatives
Encyclopedia of Careers and Vocational Guidance 2
Entrepreneur.com 102
entrepreneurs. *See* Internet store managers and entrepreneurs
exhibit sales plan 155
extension work instructors 41. *See also* college professors, sales and marketing

F

FADA. *See* Fine Art Dealers Association
"fair letters" 47
Favorite Things Antique Shop (Orland Park, IL) 13
field contractors 113. *See also* purchasing agents
financial consultants. *See* financial services brokers
Financial Industry Regulatory Authority (FINRA) 51, 56, 74, 77

financial-report service sales agents 163. *See also* service sales representatives
financial services brokers 72–77
financial specialists. *See* financial services brokers
Fine Art Dealers Association (FADA) 18
FINRA. *See* Financial Industry Regulatory Authority
floor brokers 50. *See also* commodities brokers
floor managers 53, 140. *See also* commodities brokers; retail sales workers
Ford Motor Company 29
"forward contracts" 47
freelancers. *See* self-employment
full service brokers 48. *See also* commodities brokers
Futures Magazine 52

G

general agency managers 87. *See also* insurance agents and brokers
general agents 87. *See also* insurance agents and brokers
general insurance brokers 87. *See also* insurance agents and brokers
general managers 140, 175. *See also* retail sales workers; wireless sales workers
General Motors 29
General Securities Registered Representative Examination 74
GOE. *See Guide for Occupational Exploration*
Google.com 99
graduate personal property appraiser 24
graduate personal property appraiser-master 24
grain brokers-and-market operators 114. *See also* purchasing agents
grain buyers 113–114. *See also* purchasing agents
Great Atlantic and Pacific Tea Company 128
group sales plan 155
group sales representatives 163. *See also* service sales representatives
Guide for Occupational Exploration (GOE) 2, 3

H

"hard" products 169
Harley Davidson 59

182   Careers in Focus: Sales

head tobacco buyers 113. *See also* purchasing agents
health insurance 79, 80
health maintenance organizations (HMOs) 80
The History of Marketing Thought (Bartels) 39
HMOs. *See* health maintenance organizations
holidays/events, consumer spending 131
hotel services sales representatives 163. *See also* service sales representatives
Human Resources Development Canada 3

I

ICSA Labs 111
IIABA. *See* Independent Insurance Agents and Brokers of America
Independent Insurance Agents and Brokers of America (IIABA) 84, 90
Indiana University, Certified Auctioneers Institute 23, 24
industrial relations sales agents. *See* psychological test and industrial relations sales agents
industrial sales workers 153. *See also* sales representatives
information technology (IT) 59
Information Technology Association of America 102
inside sales workers 170. *See also* wireless sales workers
Institute for Certification of Computing Professionals 98, 102
Institute for Financial Markets 51
Institute for Supply Management 112, 114, 118
Institute of Certified Professional Managers 98, 102
insurance agents and brokers 78–93
Insurance Educational Association 90
insurance industry, history of 78–79
Insurance Information Institute 90
Insurance Institute of America 89–90
Insurance Institute of Canada 91–92
Insurance Vocational Education Student Training 90
Intellefunds, Inc. (St. Louis, MO) 104
Intercontinental Exchange 57
International Auctioneer Champion 13
International Society of Appraisers (ISA) 15, 18–19

Internet, development of 94–95, 103–104
Internet sales specialists 33. *See also* automobile sales workers
Internet store managers and entrepreneurs 94–102
Internet transaction specialists 103–111
internships
  advertising account executives 11
  computer and electronics sales representatives 64
  counter and rental clerks 71
introducing brokers 50. *See also* commodities brokers
An Introduction to Futures and Options 52
ISA. *See* International Society of Appraisers
IT. *See* information technology

J

JCPenney.com 99
Jones, J. G. 39
junior college sales and marketing instructors 41. *See also* college professors, sales and marketing
Jupiter Communications 95

K

Kansas City commodity futures exchange 50
Kohls.com 99
Kopach, Marty 92–93
Kovels' Antiques & Collectibles Price List 13
Krause, Gene 104, 110
Kroger's 59

L

licensing. *See* certification and licensing
life insurance 79–80
Life Insurance Marketing and Research Association. *See* LIMRA International
LIMRA International 86, 91
Los Angeles, CA 8, 9, 25

M

managers. *See* Internet store managers and entrepreneurs; retail sales managers; sales managers
manufacturers' agents 158. *See also* sales representatives

Manufacturers' Agents National Association 160
Manufacturers' Representatives Education Research Foundation 156, 167
manufacturers' sales representatives. *See* sales representatives
manufacturers' sales workers. *See* sales representatives
Marconi, Guglielmo 168
Marketing Methods and Salesmanship (Butler, DeBower and Jones) 39
Marshall Field's department stores 136
McDonald's Corporation 146
MCI Verizon. *See* Verizon
media buyers 6. *See also* advertising account executives
Medicaid 80
Medicare 80
Merrill Lynch 50
military service. *See* U.S. armed forces
Minneapolis commodity futures exchange 50
Minneapolis Grain Exchange 57
Morgan Stanley 50

N

NAA. *See* National Auctioneers Association
NADA. *See* National Automobile Dealers Association
NAMT. *See* American Marketing Association
National Alliance for Insurance Education and Research 84
National Association of Government Purchasing 114, 118
National Association of Health Underwriters 91
National Association of Insurance and Financial Advisors 91
National Association of Marketing Teachers (NAMT). *See* American Marketing Association
National Association of Professional Insurance Agents 91
National Association of Purchasing Agents. *See* Institute for Supply Management
National Association of Real Estate Exchanges. *See* National Association of Realtors
National Association of Realtors 120, 127

National Association of Teachers of Advertising. *See* National Association of Marketing Teachers
National Auctioneers Association (NAA) 23, 24, 28
National Automobile Dealers Association (NADA) 29, 30, 34, 35, 36, 38
National Commodities Futures Examination 51, 56
National Futures Association 51, 56
National Institute of Automotive Service Excellence 35, 38
National Management Association 150
National Occupational Classification (NOC) Index 2, 3
National Retail Federation
 contact information 71, 119, 134, 142
 counter and rental clerks 68
 retail sales managers 131, 132
 retail sales workers 138
Naujokas, Sandra 13–14, 16
New Deal 30
New York City, NY 8, 9, 20, 25, 148
New York Mercantile Exchange 49, 50, 57
New York Stock Exchange 73
NOC Index. *See* National Occupational Classification Index
North American Retail Dealers Association 65
Northwestern Mutual Financial Network 92

O

O'Brien Associates, R. J. 50
Occupational Information Network (O*NET)-Standard Occupational Classification System (SOC) index 2, 3
Occupational Outlook Handbook 3, 126
Office Depot 64
O*NET-SOC index. *See* Occupational Information Network-Standard Occupational Classification System index
online auction 27
online retailers 99
online sales managers. *See* Internet store managers and entrepreneurs
"open outcry" system 54
outside sales workers 170. *See also* wireless sales workers
Overstock.com 99

P

Philadelphia Stock Exchange 56
phone clerks 53. *See also* commodities brokers
PPOs. *See* preferred provider organizations
preferred provider organizations (PPOs) 80
Price Labeling Law 30
procurement engineers 113. *See also* purchasing agents
professors. *See* college professors, sales and marketing
property and casualty insurance 79, 80–81
property managers 125. *See also* real estate agents and brokers
psychological test and industrial relations sales agents 163. *See also* service sales representatives
public utilities sales representatives 163. *See also* service sales representatives
purchase-price analysts 113. *See also* purchasing agents
purchasing agents 112–119
Purchasing magazine 115

Q

Quartermaster Corps 116
Quigley, Brian 170–171, 173, 175

R

radio, development of 168–169
real estate agents and brokers 120–127
real estate brokers. *See* real estate agents and brokers
real estate counselors 125. *See also* real estate agents and brokers
regional managers 158. *See also* sales representatives
registered representatives. *See* financial services brokers
rental clerks. *See* counter and rental clerks; retail sales workers
The Representor magazine 65
"reserved bid" 21
Retail Industry Leaders Association 71, 134, 150
retail sales managers 128–134
retail sales workers 135–144
Roosevelt, Franklin Delano 30
runners 52. *See also* commodities brokers

S

sales clerks. *See* retail sales workers
sales engineers 153. *See also* sales representatives
sales field
  books to read 43
  competition 1
  described 1–2
sales managers 145–150, 175. *See also* retail sales managers; wireless sales workers
Sales and Marketing Executives International (SME) 164, 167
salespeople. *See* retail sales workers
sales promotion representatives 163. *See also* service sales representatives
sales representatives 151–160. *See also* service sales representatives
sales reps. *See* sales representatives
sales-service promoters 162. *See also* service sales representatives
sales workers. *See* automobile sales workers; retail sales workers; wireless sales workers
SASP. *See* Society of Automotive Sales Professionals
Schroeder's Antiques Price Guide 13–14
Sears (Internet store) 96, 99
"seat" (broker membership) 50
Securities Industry and Financial Markets Association 77
securities sales representatives. *See* financial services brokers
self-employment
  auctioneers 27
  commodities brokers 52
  financial services brokers 75
  Internet store managers and entrepreneurs 96, 100, 101
  real estate agents and brokers 124, 125
  sales representatives 151
Selling Power magazine 164
semiconductor, development of 58
senior account executives 175. *See also* wireless sales workers
senior sales representatives 175. *See also* wireless sales workers
senior sales workers 140. *See also* retail sales workers
service-establishment attendants 67. *See also* counter and rental clerks
service sales representatives 161–167
Small Business Administration 99, 102

SME. *See* Sales and Marketing Executives International
Society of Automotive Sales Professionals (SASP) 36
Society of Financial Service Professionals 91
Society of Industrial and Office Realtors 127
"soft" products 169
software developers 103. *See also* Internet transaction specialists
Sotheby's (auction house) 16
Sprint Nextel 174, 175
stockbrokers. *See* financial services brokers
store managers. *See* Internet store managers and entrepreneurs
subscription crew leader 155. *See also* sales representatives

T

Target.com 99
telephone services sales representatives 163. *See also* service sales representatives
Thorness, Jeff 104–105, 106, 107, 109–110
T-Mobile 175
traders 48. *See also* commodities brokers
trainers 175. *See also* wireless sales workers
transaction specialists. *See* Internet transaction specialists
travelers' checks sales representatives 163. *See also* service sales representatives
2600 magazine 107

U

underwriters 78. *See also* insurance agents and brokers
Uniform Securities Agents State Law Examination 75
Universal Public Purchasing Certification Council 114
University of Pennsylvania 39
University of Wisconsin 39
university professors. *See* college professors, sales and marketing
U.S. Air Force 116
U.S. armed forces purchasing agents 116
U.S. Army Quartermaster Corps 116
U.S. Bureau of Labor Statistics 3
U.S. Cellular 174

U.S. Department of Labor (USDL)
 earnings data 1
  advertising account executives 9
  automobile sales workers 37
  college professors, sales and marketing 45
  commodities brokers 54
  computer and electronics sales representatives 63
  counter and rental clerks 70
  financial services brokers 76
  insurance agents and brokers 87
  Internet transaction specialists 109
  purchasing agents 117
  real estate agents and brokers 125
  retail sales managers 133
  retail sales workers 140
  sales managers 148
  sales representatives 159
  service sales representatives 166
 employers
  financial services brokers 75
 job outlook 2
  advertising account executives 10
  college professors, sales and marketing 45
  commodities brokers 54
  computer and electronics sales representatives 64
  counter and rental clerks 71
  financial services brokers 76
  insurance agents and brokers 88–89
  purchasing agents 117
  retail sales managers 134
  retail sales workers 142
  sales managers 149
  sales representatives 160
 latest information from 2
 numerical designation for career 3
 postsecondary training
  sales representatives 156
USDL. *See* U.S. Department of Labor
U.S. Navy 116
U.S. News & World Report 94, 176

V

vacuum tubes 58
Verizon 174, 175

W

Wal-Mart.com 99
Washingtonpost.com 94

watch-and-clock-repair clerks 67. *See also* counter and rental clerks
Wells, Randy 23, 24, 27
wholesale sales representatives. *See* sales representatives
wholesale trade sales workers. *See* sales representatives
wireless carriers 175
Wireless Industry Association 177
wireless sales representatives. *See* wireless sales workers
wireless sales workers 168–178
Woolworth, F. W. 128
World Wide Web. *See* Internet, development of
Wright, Dave 96–98, 100